# THE LAMBETH CONFERENCE 1968

Resolutions and Reports

# THE LAMBETH CONFERENCE 1968

# RESOLUTIONS AND REPORTS

S.P.C.K. AND
SEABURY PRESS
1968

*First published in 1968*
*by S.P.C.K.*
*Holy Trinity Church, Marylebone Road, London, N.W.1*
*and The Seabury Press*
*815 Second Avenue, New York, N.Y. 10017*

Made and printed in Great Britain by
Hazell Watson & Viney Limited, Aylesbury, Bucks

SBN (U.K.) 281 02308 5

# Contents

## PRESIDENT OF THE CONFERENCE

A. M. Ramsey
Archbishop of Canterbury

## STEERING COMMITTEE

| | |
|---|---|
| G. O. Simms | Archbishop of Dublin |
| R. W. Stopford | Bishop of London |
| R. C. Mortimer | Bishop of Exeter |
| S. A. H. Eley | Bishop of Gibraltar |
| S. F. Bayne Jr | Vice-President of the Executive Council of P E C U S A |
| R. S. Dean | Bishop of Cariboo *Episcopal Secretary* |

# Bishops attending the Lambeth Conference of 1968

## Province of Canterbury

| | |
|---|---|
| A. M. Ramsey | Primate of All England and Archbishop of Canterbury |
| R. W. Stopford | Bishop of London |
| S. F. Allison | Bishop of Winchester |
| J. L. Wilson | Bishop of Birmingham |
| E. M. Gresford Jones | Bishop of St Albans |
| G. F. Allen | Bishop of Derby |
| C. K. N. Bardsley | Bishop of Coventry |
| J. M. Key | Bishop of Truro |
| R. P. Wilson | Bishop of Chichester |
| R. C. Mortimer | Bishop of Exeter |
| W. L. C. Fleming | Bishop of Norwich |
| C. Eastaugh | Bishop of Peterborough |
| K. Riches | Bishop of Lincoln |
| A. S. Reeve | Bishop of Lichfield |
| R. R. Williams | Bishop of Leicester |
| L. W. Brown | Bishop of St Edmundsbury and Ipswich |
| H. J. Carpenter | Bishop of Oxford |
| E. B. Henderson | Bishop of Bath and Wells |
| M. A. Hodson | Bishop of Hereford |
| L. M. Charles-Edwards | Bishop of Worcester |
| E. J. K. Roberts | Bishop of Ely |
| B. T. Guy | Bishop of Gloucester |
| O. S. Tomkins | Bishop of Bristol |
| A. M. Stockwood | Bishop of Southwark |
| J. H. L. Phillips | Bishop of Portsmouth |
| R. D. Say | Bishop of Rochester |
| G. E. Reindorp | Bishop of Guildford |
| J. G. Tiarks | Bishop of Chelmsford |
| J. E. Fison | Bishop of Salisbury |
| R. N. Coote | Bishop Suffragan of Colchester |
| K. E. N. Lamplugh | Bishop Suffragan of Southampton |
| W. A. E. Westall | Bishop Suffragan of Crediton |
| J. T. Hughes | Bishop Suffragan of Croydon |
| D. G. Loveday | Bishop Suffragan of Dorchester |
| R. G. Clitherow | Bishop Suffragan of Stafford |
| W. F. P. Chadwick | Bishop Suffragan of Barking |
| A. F. B. Rogers | Bishop Suffragan of Fulham |

| | |
|---|---|
| J. A. T. ROBINSON | Bishop Suffragan of Woolwich |
| J. H. L. MORRELL | Bishop Suffragan of Lewes |
| W. A. PARKER | Bishop Suffragan of Shrewsbury |
| V. J. PIKE | Bishop Suffragan of Sherborne |
| F. T. HORAN | Bishop Suffragan of Tewkesbury |
| D. B. PORTER | Bishop Suffragan of Aston |
| F. H. WEST | Bishop Suffragan of Taunton |
| C. L. P. BISHOP | Bishop Suffragan of Malmesbury |
| W. G. SANDERSON | Bishop Suffragan of Plymouth |
| A. J. TRILLO | Bishop Suffragan of Hertford |
| W. S. LLEWELLYN | Bishop Suffragan of Lynn |
| E. W. B. CORDINGLY | Bishop Suffragan of Thetford |
| G. C. C. PEPYS | Bishop Suffragan of Buckingham |
| R. C. O. GOODCHILD | Bishop Suffragan of Kensington |
| G. D. LEONARD | Bishop Suffragan of Willesden |
| A. P. TREMLETT | Bishop Suffragan of Dover |
| R. S. HOOK | Bishop Suffragan of Grantham |
| W. W. HUNT | Bishop Suffragan of Repton |
| J. F. COLIN | Bishop Suffragan of Grimsby |
| R. A. S. MARTINEAU | Bishop Suffragan of Huntingdon |
| D. R. MADDOCK | Bishop Suffragan of Dunwich |
| J. T. H. HARE | Bishop Suffragan of Bedford |
| H. D. HALSEY | Bishop Suffragan of Tonbridge |
| W. N. WELCH | Bishop Suffragan of Bradwell |
| S. W. PHIPPS | Bishop Suffragan of Horsham |
| L. C. USHER-WILSON | Assistant Bishop of Guildford |
| D. J. WILSON | Assistant Bishop of Bath and Wells |
| A. M. HOLLIS | Assistant Bishop of St Edmundsbury and Ipswich |
| J. D. MCKIE | Assistant Bishop of Coventry |
| W. Q. LASH | Assistant Bishop of Truro |
| T. G. STUART SMITH | Assistant Bishop of Leicester |
| A. R. GRAHAM-CAMPBELL | Assistant Bishop of Peterborough |
| G. SINKER | Assistant Bishop of Birmingham |
| R. A. REEVES | Assistant Bishop of Chichester |
| L. H. WOOLMER | Assistant Bishop of Portsmouth |
| N. E. CORNWALL | Assistant Bishop of Winchester |
| T. R. PARFITT | Assistant Bishop of Derby |
| W. A. PARTRIDGE | Assistant Bishop of Hereford |
| J. K. RUSSELL | Assistant Bishop of Rochester |
| ST J. PIKE | Assistant Bishop of Guildford |
| C. K. SANSBURY | Assistant Bishop of London |
| E. J. TRAPP | General Secretary of the United Society for the Propagation of the Gospel |

*Province of York*

| | |
|---|---|
| F. D. COGGAN | Primate of England and Archbishop of York |
| I. T. RAMSEY | Bishop of Durham |
| C. R. CLAXTON | Bishop of Blackburn |
| W. D. L. GREER | Bishop of Manchester |
| G. A. ELLISON | Bishop of Chester |
| C. G. ST M. PARKER | Bishop of Bradford |
| H. E. ASHDOWN | Bishop of Newcastle |
| S. C. BULLEY | Bishop of Carlisle |
| J. R. H. MOORMAN | Bishop of Ripon |
| G. D. SAVAGE | Bishop of Southwell |
| E. TREACY | Bishop of Wakefield |
| F. J. TAYLOR | Bishop of Sheffield |
| S. Y. BLANCH | Bishop of Liverpool |
| G. E. GORDON | Bishop of Sodor and Man |
| K. V. RAMSEY | Bishop Suffragan of Hulme |
| G. E. HOLDERNESS | Bishop Suffragan of Burnley |
| A. L. E. HOSKYNS-ABRAHALL | Bishop Suffragan of Lancaster |
| E. R. WICKHAM | Bishop Suffragan of Middleton |
| L. A. BROWN | Bishop Suffragan of Warrington |
| G. D'O. SNOW | Bishop Suffragan of Whitby |
| D. N. SARGENT | Bishop Suffragan of Selby |
| A. K. HAMILTON | Bishop Suffragan of Jarrow |
| H. L. HIGGS | Bishop Suffragan of Hull |
| J. H. CRUSE | Bishop Suffragan of Knaresborough |
| K. G. THOMPSON | Bishop Suffragan of Sherwood |
| E. A. J. MERCER | Bishop Suffragan of Birkenhead |
| R. G. STRUTT | Bishop Suffragan of Stockport |
| R. FOSKETT | Bishop Suffragan of Penrith |
| W. G. FALLOWS | Bishop Suffragan of Pontefract |
| G. V. GERARD | Assistant Bishop of Sheffield |
| V. G. SHEARBURN | Assistant Bishop of Wakefield |

*Wales*

| | |
|---|---|
| W. G. H. SIMON | Archbishop of Wales and Bishop of Llandaff |
| D. D. BARTLETT | Bishop of St Asaph |
| J. R. RICHARDS | Bishop of St Davids |
| G. O. WILLIAMS | Bishop of Bangor |
| J. J. A. THOMAS | Bishop of Swansea and Brecon |
| E. S. THOMAS | Bishop of Monmouth |

*Ireland*

| | |
|---|---|
| J. McCann | Primate of All Ireland and Archbishop of Armagh |
| G. O. Simms | Primate of Ireland and Archbishop of Dublin |
| R. B. Pike | Bishop of Meath |
| F. J. Mitchell | Bishop of Down and Dromore |
| R. G. Perdue | Bishop of Cork, Cloyne, and Ross |
| C. J. Tyndall | Bishop of Derry and Raphoe |
| R. C. H. G. Elliott | Bishop of Connor |
| H. A. Stanistreet | Bishop of Killaloe and Kilfenora, Clonfert and Kilmacduagh |
| A. H. Butler | Bishop of Tuam, Killala, and Achonry |
| A. A. Buchanan | Bishop of Clogher |
| E. F. Moore | Bishop of Kilmore and Elphin and Ardagh |
| R. W. Jackson | Bishop of Limerick, Ardfert, and Aghadoe |
| H. R. McAdoo | Bishop of Ossory, Ferns, and Leighlin |

*Scotland*

| | |
|---|---|
| F. H. Moncreiff | Primus of the Scottish Episcopal Church and Bishop of Glasgow and Galloway |
| D. Macinnes | Bishop of Moray, Ross, and Caithness |
| J. W. A. Howe | Bishop of St Andrews, Dunkeld, and Dunblane |
| E. F. Easson | Bishop of Aberdeen and Orkney |
| J. C. Sprott | Bishop of Brechin |
| K. M. Carey | Bishop of Edinburgh |
| R. K. Wimbush | Bishop of Argyll and the Isles |

*United States of America*

| | |
|---|---|
| J. E. Hines | Presiding Bishop of the Protestant Episcopal Church of the United States of America |
| S. F. Bayne Jr | Vice-Chairman of the Executive Council and Director of the Overseas Department of PECUSA |
| D. Corrigan | Director of the Home Department of the Executive Council of PECUSA |
| C. C. J. Carpenter | Bishop of Alabama |

| | |
|---|---|
| W. H. GRAY | Bishop of Connecticut |
| C. A. VOEGELI | Bishop of Haiti |
| H. S. KENNEDY | Bishop of Honolulu |
| A. PARDUE | Bishop of Pittsburgh |
| W. W. HORSTICK | Bishop of Eau Claire |
| C. H. GESNER | Bishop of South Dakota |
| R. H. GOODEN | Bishop of Panama and the Canal Zone |
| H. I. LOUTTIT | Bishop of South Florida |
| C. A. MASON | Bishop of Dallas |
| T. H. WRIGHT | Bishop of East Carolina |
| W. R. MOODY | Bishop of Lexington |
| L. W. BARTON | Bishop of Eastern Oregon |
| G. H. QUARTERMAN | Bishop of Northwest Texas |
| H. W. B. DONEGAN | Bishop of New York |
| J. W. HUNTER | Bishop of Wyoming |
| F. E. I. BLOY | Bishop of Los Angeles |
| L. L. SCAIFE | Bishop of Western New York |
| W. J. GORDON JR | Bishop of Alaska |
| M. G. HENRY | Bishop of Western North Carolina |
| E. H. WEST | Bishop of Florida |
| W. M. HIGLEY | Bishop of Central New York |
| J. G. SHERMAN | Bishop of Long Island |
| G. M. JONES | Bishop of Louisiana |
| R. R. CLAIBORNE JR | Bishop of Atlanta |
| R. F. GIBSON | Bishop of Virginia |
| E. R. WELLES | Bishop of West Missouri |
| G. V. SMITH | Bishop of Iowa |
| W. C. CAMPBELL | Bishop of West Virginia |
| G. F. BURRILL | Bishop of Chicago |
| R. S. WATSON | Bishop of Utah |
| C. POWELL | Bishop of Oklahoma |
| D. H. V. HALLOCK | Bishop of Milwaukee |
| H. H. KELLOGG | Bishop of Minnesota |
| W. CRITTENDEN | Bishop of Erie |
| J. S. HIGGINS | Bishop of Rhode Island |
| F. J. WARNECKE | Bishop of Bethlehem |
| W. H. BRADY | Bishop of Fond du Lac |
| L. STARK | Bishop of Newark |
| C. J. KINSOLVING III | Bishop of New Mexico and Southwest Texas |
| J. B. MOSLEY | Bishop of Delaware |
| C. G. MARMION | Bishop of Kentucky |
| W. H. MARMION | Bishop of Southwestern Virginia |
| J. J. M. HARTE | Bishop of Arizona |
| A. R. STUART | Bishop of Georgia |
| J. V. HORST | Bishop of Tennessee |

| | |
|---|---|
| H. L. Doll | Bishop of Maryland |
| R. R. Brown | Bishop of Arkansas |
| J. W. F. Carman | Bishop of Oregon |
| E. C. Turner | Bishop of Kansas |
| C. R. Haden Jr | Bishop of Northern California |
| F. W. Lickfield | Bishop of Quincy |
| A. W. Brown | Bishop of Albany |
| G. L. Cadigan | Bishop of Missouri |
| W. F. Creighton | Bishop of Washington |
| C. E. Bennison | Bishop of Western Michigan |
| P. A. Kellogg | Bishop of Dominican Republic |
| I. I. Curtis | Bishop of Olympia |
| T. A. Fraser Jr | Bishop of North Carolina |
| G. Temple | Bishop of South Carolina |
| H. D. Butterfield | Bishop of Vermont |
| R. T. Rauscher | Bishop of Nebraska |
| J. M. Allin | Bishop of Mississippi |
| A. A. Chambers | Bishop of Springfield |
| C. E. Mills | Bishop of Virgin Islands |
| G. W. Barrett | Bishop of Rochester |
| W. C. Klein | Bishop of Northern Indiana |
| J. A. Pinckney | Bishop of Upper South Carolina |
| D. B. Reed | Bishop of Colombia and Ecuador |
| C. K. Myers | Bishop of California |
| G. R. Selway | Bishop of Northern Michigan |
| F. Reus-Froylan | Bishop of Puerto Rico |
| G. T. Masuda | Bishop of North Dakota |
| J. M. Richardson | Bishop of Texas |
| W. Davidson | Bishop of Western Kansas |
| G. A. Taylor | Bishop of Easton |
| J. H. Burt | Bishop of Ohio |
| J. R. Wyatt | Bishop of Spokane |
| W. C. Frey | Bishop of Guatemala and El Salvador |
| E. L. Browning | Bishop of Okinawa |
| I. B. Noland | Bishop Coadjutor of Louisiana |
| G. M. Murray | Bishop Coadjutor of Alabama |
| D. S. Rose | Bishop Coadjutor of Southern Virginia |
| W. E. Sanders | Bishop Coadjutor of Tennessee |
| J. W. Montgomery | Bishop Coadjutor of Chicago |
| R. B. Hall | Bishop Coadjutor of Virginia |
| C. Keller | Bishop Coadjutor of Arkansas |
| R. B. Appleyard | Bishop Coadjutor of Pittsburgh |
| H. B. Robinson | Bishop Coadjutor of Western New York |
| A. Crowley | Bishop Suffragan of Michigan |
| R. E. Dicus | Bishop Suffragan of West Texas |

| | |
|---|---|
| F. P. GODDARD | Bishop Suffragan of Texas |
| A. M. LEWIS | Bishop Suffragan of the Armed Forces |
| P. F. McNAIRY | Bishop Suffragan of Minnesota |
| J. S. WETMORE | Bishop Suffragan of New York |
| G. R. MILLARD | Bishop Suffragan of California |
| S. B. CHILTON | Bishop Suffragan of Virginia |
| J. L. DUNCAN | Bishop Suffragan of South Florida |
| W. L. HARGRAVE | Bishop Suffragan of South Florida |
| C. W. McLEAN | Bishop Suffragan of Long Island |
| J. M. BURGESS | Bishop Suffragan of Massachusetts |
| C. B. PERSELL JR | Bishop Suffragan of Albany |
| F. PUTNAM JR | Bishop Suffragan of Oklahoma |
| L. R. ROMERO | Bishop Suffragan of Mexico |
| M. SAUCEDO | Bishop Suffragan of Mexico |
| S. F. BAILEY | Bishop Suffragan of Texas |
| R. C. RUSACK | Bishop Suffragan of Los Angeles |
| H. R. GROSS | Bishop Suffragan of Oregon |
| A. W. VAN DUZER | Bishop Suffragan of New Jersey |
| W. F. GATES JR | Bishop Suffragan of Tennessee |
| W. P. BARNDS | Bishop Suffragan of Dallas |
| R. B. MARTIN | Bishop Suffragan of Long Island |
| R. R. SPEARS | Bishop Suffragan of West Missouri |
| M. L. WOOD | Bishop Suffragan of Atlanta |
| E. McNAIR | Bishop Suffragan of Northern California |
| E. L. HANCHETT | Bishop Suffragan of Honolulu |
| A. E. SWIFT | Assistant Bishop in South Florida |
| A. TSU | Consultant Bishop in Pennsylvania |
| D. CAMPBELL | |

## Canada

| | |
|---|---|
| H. H. CLARK | Primate of All Canada, Archbishop and Metropolitan of Rupert's Land |
| W. L. WRIGHT | Archbishop of Algoma and Metropolitan of Ontario |
| A. H. O'NEIL | Archbishop of Fredericton and Metropolitan of the Province of Canada |
| G. P. GOWER | Archbishop of New Westminster and Metropolitan of British Columbia |

| | |
|---|---|
| H. E. SEXTON | Bishop of British Columbia |
| G. N. LUXTON | Bishop of Huron |
| W. E. BAGNALL | Bishop of Niagara |
| I. A. NORRIS | Bishop of Brandon |
| D. B. MARSH | Bishop of the Arctic |
| S. C. STEER | Bishop of Saskatoon |
| R. J. PIERCE | Bishop of Athabasca |
| K. C. EVANS | Bishop of Ontario |
| H. E. HIVES | Bishop of Keewatin |
| E. S. REED | Bishop of Ottawa |
| G. B. SNELL | Bishop of Toronto |
| R. S. DEAN | Bishop of Cariboo, Anglican Executive Officer and Episcopal Secretary |
| W. W. DAVIS | Bishop of Nova Scotia |
| R. L. SEABORN | Bishop of Newfoundland |
| E. G. MUNN | Bishop of Caledonia |
| W. H. N. CRUMP | Bishop of Saskatchewan |
| W. G. BURCH | Bishop of Edmonton |
| G. F. C. JACKSON | Bishop of Qu'Appelle |
| R. F. BROWN | Bishop of Quebec |
| R. K. MAGUIRE | Bishop of Montreal |
| J. A. WATTON | Bishop of Moosonee |
| E. W. SCOTT | Bishop of Kootenay |
| M. L. GOODMAN | Bishop of Calgary |
| J. T. FRAME | Bishop of Yukon |
| J. O. ANDERSON | Bishop Coadjutor of Rupert's Land |
| N. R. CLARKE | Bishop Suffragan of James Bay |
| H. R. HUNT | Bishop Suffragan of Toronto |
| H. F. G. APPLEYARD | Bishop Suffragan of Georgian Bay |
| H. G. COOK | Bishop Suffragan of Athabasca |
| C. J. QUEEN | Bishop Suffragan of St Clair |
| G. F. ARNOLD | Bishop Suffragan of Nova Scotia |
| W. C. LEGGE | Bishop Suffragan of Newfoundland |
| C. H. R. WILKINSON | Assistant Bishop of Niagara |
| T. GREENWOOD | Assistant Bishop of Cariboo |

*India, Pakistan, Burma, and Ceylon*

| | |
|---|---|
| H. L. J. DE MEL | Metropolitan of India, Pakistan, Burma, and Ceylon and Bishop of Calcutta |
| C. J. G. ROBINSON | Bishop of Bombay |

| | |
|---|---|
| J. Amritanand | Bishop of Lucknow |
| R. W. Bryan | Bishop of Barrackpore |
| J. D. Blair | Bishop of Dacca |
| P. Parmar | Bishop of Delhi |
| C. Ray | Bishop of Karachi |
| J. W. Sadiq | Bishop of Nagpur |
| A. W. Luther | Bishop of Nasik |
| S. A. B. Dilbar Hans | Bishop of Chota Nagpur |
| E. S. Nasir | Bishop of Amritsar |
| C. L. Wickremesinghe | Bishop of Kurunagala |
| C. H. W. de Soysa | Bishop of Colombo |
| M. D. Srinivasan | Bishop of Andaman and Nicobar Islands |
| E. John | Bishop of Nandyal |
| A. V. Jonathan | Bishop of Assam |
| I. Masih | Bishop of Lahore |

*Australia*

| | |
|---|---|
| P. N. W. Strong | Primate of Australia, Archbishop of Brisbane and Metropolitan of Queensland |
| F. Woods | Archbishop of Melbourne and Metropolitan of Victoria |
| G. Appleton | Archbishop of Perth and Metropolitan of West Australia |
| M. L. Loane | Archbishop of Sydney and Metropolitan of New South Wales |
| J. A. G. Housden | Bishop of Newcastle |
| K. J. Clements | Bishop of Canberra and Goulburn |
| G. D. Hand | Bishop of New Guinea |
| A. E. Winter | Bishop of St Arnaud |
| I. W. A. Shevill | Bishop of North Queensland |
| R. C. Kerle | Bishop of Armidale |
| R. G. Arthur | Bishop of Grafton |
| R. E. Richards | Bishop of Bendigo |
| T. T. Reed | Bishop of Adelaide |
| R. G. Hawkins | Bishop of Bunbury |
| T. E. Jones | Bishop of Willochra |
| E. K. Leslie | Bishop of Bathurst |
| D. A. Garnsey | Bishop of Gippsland |
| T. B. McCall | Bishop of Wangaratta |
| R. E. Davies | Bishop of Tasmania |
| W. A. Hardie | Bishop of Ballarat |
| D. N. Shearman | Bishop of Rockhampton |

| | |
|---|---|
| H. A. J. WITT | Bishop of North West Australia |
| J. B. R. GRINDROD | Bishop of Riverina |
| D. W. BRYANT | Bishop of Kalgoorlie |
| K. B. MASON | Bishop of Northern Territory |
| E. E. HAWKEY | Bishop of Carpentaria |
| F. O. HULME-MOIR | Bishop Coadjutor of Sydney |
| G. T. SAMBELL | Bishop Coadjutor of Melbourne |
| G. AMBO | Assistant Bishop of New Guinea |

*New Zealand*

| | |
|---|---|
| N. A. LESSER | Primate and Archbishop of New Zealand and Bishop of Waiapu |
| H. W. BAINES | Bishop of Wellington |
| J. T. HOLLAND | Bishop of Waikato |
| A. H. JOHNSTON | Bishop of Dunedin |
| J. C. VOCKLER | Bishop in Polynesia |
| E. A. GOWING | Bishop of Auckland |
| J. W. CHISHOLM | Bishop of Melanesia |
| P. E. SUTTON | Bishop of Nelson |
| W. A. PYATT | Bishop of Christchurch |
| F. HALAPUA | Bishop Suffragan of Nuku'alofa |

*South Africa*

| | |
|---|---|
| R. S. TAYLOR | Metropolitan of South Africa and Archbishop of Cape Town |
| L. E. STRADLING | Bishop of Johannesburg |
| J. A. A. MAUND | Bishop of Lesotho |
| T. G. V. INMAN | Bishop of Natal |
| P. W. WHEELDON | Bishop of Kimberley and Kuruman |
| J. L. SCHUSTER | Bishop of St John's |
| E. G. KNAPP-FISHER | Bishop of Pretoria |
| R. H. MIZE | Bishop of Damaraland |
| A. H. ZULU | Bishop of Zululand and Swaziland |
| G. L. TINDALL | Bishop of Grahamstown |
| P. H. F. BARRON | Bishop of George |
| D. DE P. CABRAL | Bishop of Lebombo |
| F. A. AMOORE | Bishop of Bloemfontein |
| E. M. H. CAPPER | Bishop of St Helena |
| P. W. R. RUSSELL | Bishop Suffragan of Cape Town |
| F. MAKHETHA | Bishop Suffragan of Lesotho |

B. B. BURNETT                   General Secretary of the Christian
                                Council of South Africa

### West Indies

A. J. KNIGHT                    Archbishop of the West Indies
                                and Bishop of Guyana
W. J. HUGHES                    Bishop of Trinidad and Tobago
D. R. KNOWLES                   Bishop of Antigua
E. L. EVANS                     Bishop of Barbados
J. C. E. SWABY                  Bishop of Jamaica
B. N. Y. VAUGHAN                Bishop of British Honduras
B. MARKHAM                      Bishop of Nassau and the
                                Bahamas
P. E. R. ELDER                  Bishop Suffragan of Stabroek
G. MARSHALL                     Bishop Suffragan in Venezuela

### Japan

D. M. GOTO                      Bishop of Tokyo
M. T. KOIKE                     Bishop of Osaka
K. VIALL                        Assistant Bishop of Tokyo

### West Africa

C. J. PATTERSON                 Archbishop of West Africa and
                                Bishop on the Niger
S. O. ODUTOLA                   Bishop of Ibadan
J. E. L. MORT                   Bishop of Northern Nigeria
G. E. I. COCKIN                 Bishop of Owerri
M. N. C. O. SCOTT               Bishop of Sierra Leone
R. N. BARA-HART                 Bishop of the Niger Delta
A. IWE                          Bishop of Benin
S. I. KALE                      Bishop of Lagos
I. O. S. OKUNSANYA              Bishop of Ondo
T. O. OLUFOSOYE                 Bishop of The Gambia and The
                                Rio Pongas
M. A. OSANYIN                   Bishop of Ekiti
P. J. JONES                     Assistant Bishop of Sierra Leone
H. I. A. AFONYA                 Assistant Bishop of the Niger
                                Delta
L. M. UZODIKE                   Assistant Bishop on the Niger
I. S. M. LEMAIRE                Assistant Bishop of Accra

| I. G. A. Jadesimi | Assistant Bishop of Ibadan |
| J. B. Arthur | Assistant Bishop of Accra |
| A. K. Nelson | Assistant Bishop of Accra |
| B. C. Nwankiti | Assistant Bishop of Owerri |

## Central Africa

| F. O. Green-Wilkinson | Archbishop of Central Africa and Bishop of Zambia |
| D. S. Arden | Bishop of Malawi |
| K. J. F. Skelton | Bishop of Matabeleland |
| J. P. Burrough | Bishop of Mashonaland |
| F. Mataka | Bishop Suffragan of Zambia |
| J. Mtekateka | Bishop Suffragan of Malawi |

## Jerusalem Archbishopric

| A. C. MacInnes | Archbishop in Jerusalem |
| O. C. Allison | Bishop in The Sudan |
| J. A. Cuba'in | Bishop in Jordan, Lebanon, and Syria |
| H. Dehqani-Tafti | Bishop in Iran |
| Y. Dotiro | Assistant Bishop in The Sudan |
| E. J. Ngalamu | Assistant Bishop in The Sudan |

## East Africa

| L. J. Beecher | Archbishop of East Africa and Bishop of Nairobi |
| A. Stanway | Bishop of Central Tanganyika |
| F. H. Olang' | Bishop of Maseno |
| O. Kariuki | Bishop of Mount Kenya |
| M. L. Wiggins | Bishop of Victoria Nyanza |
| N. Langford-Smith | Bishop of Nakuru |
| E. U. T. Huddleston | Bishop of Masasi |
| J. R. W. Poole-Hughes | Bishop of Southwest Tanganyika |
| M. Kahuranaga | Bishop of Western Tanganyika |
| J. Sepeku | Bishop of Dar-es-Salaam |
| P. Mwang'ombe | Bishop of Mombasa |
| G. Chitemo | Bishop of Morogoro |
| Y. Jumaa | Bishop of Zanzibar and Tanga |
| R. N. Russell | Assistant Bishop of Zanzibar and Tanga |

| | |
|---|---|
| M. D. SOSELEJE | Assistant Bishop of Masasi |
| Y. MADINDA | Assistant Bishop of Central Tanganyika |
| J. W. MLELE | Assistant Bishop of Southwest Tanganyika |
| E. J. AGOLA | Assistant Bishop of Maseno |

*Uganda, Rwanda, and Burundi*

| | |
|---|---|
| E. SABITI | Archbishop of Uganda, Rwanda, and Burundi and Bishop of Ruwenzori |
| S. S. TOMUSANGE | Bishop of West Buganda |
| K. SHALITA | Bishop of Ankole |
| D. K. NSUBUGA | Bishop of Namirembe |
| S. WANI | Bishop of Northern Uganda |
| E. K. MASABA | Bishop of Mbale |
| Y. NKUNZUMWAMI | Bishop of Burundi |
| A. SEBUNUNGURI | Bishop of Rwanda |
| A. MARAKA | Bishop of Soroti |
| R. E. LYTH | Bishop of Kigezi |
| Y. K. RWAKAIKARA | Assistant Bishop of Ruwenzori |

*Brazil*

| | |
|---|---|
| E. M. KRISCHKE | Primate of the Episcopal Church of Brazil and Bishop of Southern Brazil |
| P. L. SIMOES | Bishop of Southwestern Brazil |
| E. K. SHERRILL | Bishop of Central Brazil |

*South-East Asia*

| | |
|---|---|
| J. C. L. WONG | Chairman of the Council of the Church of Southeast Asia and Bishop of Taiwan |
| R. P. C. KOH | Bishop of Jesselton (Sabah) |
| B. C. CABANBAN | Bishop of the Philippines |
| D. H. N. ALLENBY | Bishop of Kuching |
| P. LEE | Bishop of Seoul |
| C. R. RUTT | Bishop of Taejon |
| CHIU BAN IT | Bishop of Singapore and Malaya |
| J. G. H. BAKER | Bishop of Hong Kong |
| E. G. LONGID | Bishop Suffragan of the Philippines |

*Cuba*
J. A. GONZALEZ          Bishop of Cuba


*Overseas Bishops in the Canterbury Jurisdiction*

J. MARCEL          Bishop in Madagascar
S. ELEY          Bishop of Gibraltar
J. ARMSTRONG          Bishop of Bermuda
C. J. TUCKER          Bishop in Argentina and Eastern
          South America with the Falkland
          Islands
K. W. HOWELL          Bishop in Chile, Bolivia, and
          Peru
E. E. CURTIS          Bishop of Mauritius
J. SETH          Assistant Bishop in Madagascar

# Record of Events

*Thursday 25 July*
3 p.m.     Opening Service in Canterbury Cathedral

*Sunday 28 July*
10.30 a.m.    Sung Eucharist in Westminster Abbey

*Monday 19 August*
7 p.m.     Holy Communion in Thanksgiving for the Progress of the Gospel, at White City Stadium

*Sunday 25 August*
10.30 a.m.    Closing Service in St Paul's Cathedral

The business of the Conference began on Saturday 27 July with the policy addresses of the three Section Chairmen. During the following week the Conference met in thirty-three Subcommittees whose findings were considered by the respective Sections on Friday 2 August. Preliminary reports from each Section were before the Conference in plenary session on Wednesday to Friday, 7–9 August. During the following week Sectional groups (combinations of Subcommittees) worked on drafts of Section reports. These were finally approved by the Sections on Friday 16 August and presented to the Conference in plenary session on Tuesday to Saturday, 20–24 August, at which time the Resolutions on the subjects of the Section reports were passed.

Matters not on the agenda were considered on Monday and Tuesday 5 and 6 August and again on Tuesday 20 August, and a number of Resolutions arose from these discussions.

# A Message

At the end of our Conference we thank God for the renewal of fellowship and vision which he has given us as we have worked and prayed together.

Our gathering has been set against a background of grim events in Vietnam, West Africa, and Czechoslovakia, and of mounting protest against social injustice. We live in a world which will no longer accept widespread want and poverty; a world in which inherited institutions and traditional ways of thought are increasingly questioned. Even in the realm of theology, the familiar teaching through which ordinary Christians learned their faith is being re-examined and in part rejected by some theologians.

## Faith

To those bewildered by all this we say: *God is.* We believe in him and in his Son Jesus Christ, the same yesterday, today, and for ever. *God reigns.* He is the creator of all that is; he is at work throughout his creation. *God loves.* This world—torn and distracted though it is—is his world; God has not abdicated. *God speaks.* All these human conflicts and these changes are not out of his control; some of them Christians should welcome. And by the example and standards given us by his Son we judge, under the guidance of the Holy Spirit, what in this strange world is to be accepted and what rejected. We are confident that through encounter with the world and its needs expressions of our faith will be found which will speak with meaning to men today.

The faith of the Church that God reigns and loves and speaks is sustained and renewed in its members by constant prayer. Its life is in Christ and its life is vigorous as its members try to live in and with Christ. We call all Christians to fresh efforts to deepen their prayer life, to search for those forms of prayer which are most relevant to them in their own situation, and to develop that talent for stillness in the presence of God which all possess in some degree. We seek in all things to follow the Lord's example. The Lord withdrew for prayer and took his disciples with him. From prayer he and they returned to their service in the world.

## Ministry

The role of the Church in the world is the role of her Lord: that of the suffering servant. To this theme of the servant Church we found ourselves returning again and again. The impatient protests of young men and women drove home to us that the Church will be renewed only in so far as she pursues that role. We have to confess that all too often we have failed to serve as our Lord served. Consequently, to many men and women inside and outside, the Church too often appears as a self-centred or inward-looking sheltered and privileged institution. The test of every penny we spend, of every meeting we attend, and of every service we hold, is whether it makes it easier for Jesus to be seen as Lord and the Church as his servant. We call on the bishops and clergy to be vigilant against all temptations to worldliness and to strive to attain to that simplicity of living which is so evident in the life of our Lord.

The ministry, the service, of the Church to the world is and must be discharged mainly by the laity. We have given much thought to the ministry of the laity, what it is, and how it may be strengthened. The ministry of the laity does not consist solely in service to the Church or in the Church's worship. It also demands witness to the Christian gospel through word and deed in the world. The gospel is a proclamation of God's love for all men and of his will that all men should be one in the family of the children of God. It is, therefore, a gospel of reconciliation. The ministry of laypeople is that they should be agents of reconciliation. In the home, at work, in industrial disputes, in the exercise of economic power whether as employers or employed, in the bitterly divisive issues of race, it is for the laity to bring to bear a Christian influence towards social justice, compassion, and peace.

In discharging their ministry in the world, the laity must be continuously renewed and strengthened by the assembling of themselves together in the house of God for corporate worship, to hear the word of God and to receive sacramental grace. The first duty of the ordained clergy is to make provision for this. The laity have a right to expect from the clergy help and teaching on the meaning of the Christian faith and on the practice of prayer. No less do they expect mutual encouragement and sympathy when facing the question of what Christians should do in a particular situation. They have a right to a proper share in the government of the Church, so that any decisions taken may be such as will make the fulfilling of their mission in the world easier and not more difficult. Here, the voice of the younger generation, with all its vigour, enthusiasm, and idealism, must be given opportunities of expression.

*Unity*
Christians cannot properly fulfil their ministry in a disunited Church. Even now, in spite of our divisions, it would be easier if whatever can

be done together should be done together. We urge, therefore, that more attention be paid to local Councils of Churches; that all efforts to remedy social injustices, whether at national or local level, should be done ecumenically so that the world may plainly see that what is being done is being done not by this or that Christian denomination but by "the Christians". But even this is a poor substitute for a reunited Church, the one, holy, catholic, apostolic Church. Renewal demands unity: unity cannot come without renewal. Much progress towards reunion has been made, for which we thank God. Much more work remains to be done, for which we pray God's help and guidance.

Our message is a message of hope. God is active in his world. The changes which bewilder are not all evil, though all challenge us to find the right human response. God is active in his Church, renewing it so that the Church may more clearly proclaim its faith to the world, more effectively discharge its mission of service to the world, and may recover that unity for which our Lord prayed and without which it cannot be truly itself. It is for us to recognize the signs of his renewing action and to welcome them and obey them. It is no time for either despair or doubt. Rather it is a time to remember the Lord's saying, "Be of good cheer; I have overcome the world".

**THE RESOLUTIONS**
formally adopted by the Conference

## NOTE

Only the results of voting after divisions (taken at the request of the Conference) are recorded.

The function of the Conference being consultative and advisory, its findings are not to be interpreted as having legislative force throughout the Anglican Communion. No Resolution of the Lambeth Conference is binding upon any part of the Anglican Communion unless and until it has been adopted by the appropriate canonical authority.

# The Resolutions

## Section Reports

1. The Conference, without committing itself to the endorsement of the Section reports, commends them to the continuing study of the Church as statements of the views of the bishops concerned.

## Faith in the Living God

2. The Conference, having considered and welcomed
   (a) the increasing extent of human knowledge,
   (b) the prospect of human control of the natural environment,
   (c) the searching inquiries of theologians,

calls the Church to a faith in the living God which is adventurous, expectant, calm, and confident, and to faith in the standards of Christ, who was, and is, and is to come, as the criterion of what is to be welcomed and what is to be resisted in contemporary society.

3. The Conference recommends that theologians be encouraged to continue to explore fresh ways of understanding God's revelation of himself in Christ, expressed in language that makes sense in our time. It believes that this requires of the theologian respect for tradition and, of the Church, respect for freedom of inquiry.

## The Contemporary Life of Prayer

4. The Conference affirms that the primary task of the Church is to glorify God by leading all mankind into life in Christ, and that this always involves a continuous advance in the practice of prayer in the Spirit; and therefore calls upon the clergy and laity of the whole Anglican Communion to join with the bishops in their determination, in humble and penitent dependence upon God, to deepen and strengthen their life of prayer, remembering always that our Lord's periods of withdrawal for prayer were a prelude and preparation for his further service in the world that the Father might be glorified.

To this end the Church should search to discover those forms of spirituality and methods of prayer, both corporate and personal, which meet the needs of men and women today, such as those expressed by Abbé Michel Quoist in his book *Prayers of Life*. The Church should pay more attention to the development of that capacity for silent prayer which exists in all her members, and should encourage corporate and personal waiting upon God.

## Religious Communities

5. The Conference recognizes with gratitude the contribution of the Religious Communities, both of men and of women, to the life of the Church, and values their witness to the absolute character of the claims of God on the life of man, to the fruitfulness of a life given to prayer and service, and to the unity of the Church across the divisions which at present exist. It calls upon the Communities to take their part in the present renewal of the Church, in particular by seeking to renew themselves according to the priorities of the gospel and the original intention of their foundation. It recommends that, in all provinces where Communities exist, close co-operation between the bishops and the Communities should be maintained and developed.

## Man's Stewardship of Nature

6. The Conference urges all Christians, in obedience to the doctrine of creation, to take all possible action to ensure man's responsible stewardship over nature; in particular in his relationship with animals, and with regard to the conservation of soil, and the prevention of the pollution of air, soil, and ocean.

## Conservation of the Seabed

7. The Conference endorses the initiative of Dr Pardo, leader of the Maltese delegation at the United Nations, urging that steps be taken to draft a treaty embodying the following principles:

That the seabed beyond the limits of present national jurisdiction

(a) be conserved against appropriation by nations or their nationals, so that the deep ocean floor should not be allowed to become a stage for competing claims of national sovereignty;

(b) be explored in a manner consistent with the principles and purposes of the charter of the United Nations;

(c) be exploited economically or made use of with the aim of safeguarding the interests of mankind;

(d) be conserved exclusively for peaceful purposes in perpetuity.

*War*

8.   This Conference

(*a*)   reaffirms the words of the Conference of 1930 that "war as a method of settling international disputes is incompatible with the teaching and example of our Lord Jesus Christ".

(*b*)   states emphatically that it condemns the use of nuclear and bacteriological weapons.

(*c*)   holds that it is the concern of the Church

(i)   to uphold and extend the right of conscientious objection

(ii)   to oppose persistently the claim that total war or the use of weapons however ruthless or indiscriminate can be justified by results.

(*d*)   urges upon Christians the duty to support international action either through the United Nations or otherwise to settle disputes justly without recourse to war; to work towards the abolition of the competitive supply of armaments; and to develop adequate machinery for the keeping of a just and permanent peace.

*Human Unity*

9.   The Conference affirms that human unity can only be achieved if all governments are willing to work towards a form of world government designed to serve the interests of all mankind.

*Consultation Regarding World Peace*

10.   The Conference invites the Archbishop of Canterbury on its behalf to consult with the Pope and the Ecumenical Patriarch and the Praesidium of the World Council of Churches on the possibility of approaching leaders of the other world religions with a view to convening a conference at which in concert they would speak in the interests of humanity on behalf of world peace.

*Christianity and Other Faiths*

11.   It is the conviction of the Conference that, in their obedience to Christ's mission and command and in their obligation towards the contemporary world, the Christian Churches must endeavour such

positive relationship to the different religions of men, and to the doubt and denial of faith, as will

(a) set forward the common unity of mankind and a common participation in its present history;

(b) encourage Christians to increasing co-operation with men of other faiths in the fields of economic, social, and moral action;

(c) call Christians not only to study other faiths in their own seriousness but also to study unbelief in its real quality.

## Religious Dialogue

12.　The Conference recommends a renewed and vigorous implementation of the task of inter-religious dialogue already set in hand in the study centres organized by the World Council of Churches and other bodies, and urges increased Anglican support both in the seconding of personnel and in the provision of money. It also commends similar assistance for dialogue with Marxists and those who profess no religious faith.

## The Christians of the Southern Sudan

13.　The Conference wishes to place on record its gratitude to God for the faith and courage of the Christians of the Southern Sudan during the past years of testing of the Church.

The Conference sends to them and to the many thousands of their fellow Sudanese the assurance that in their suffering and the loss of homes and schools, hospitals and churches, they are not forgotten in our prayers.

The Conference rejoices to know of the tireless efforts of the Sudanese clergy, evangelists, teachers, and other church workers in their task of proclaiming the gospel of reconciliation, both in the refugee areas and in the heart of the countryside.

The Conference prays Almighty God to lead the responsible authorities speedily to find a just and lasting solution to the existing problem.

## West Africa

14.　The Conference receives the Statement from the Bishops of the Province of West Africa (p. 50) with deep thankfulness for the Christian spirit of compassion and reconciliation that informs it. It has been deeply distressed by the prolonged conflict which has divided the peoples of Nigeria and of the former Eastern Region, and which has brought, even in the days in which the Conference has been meeting, death through starvation and disease to so many innocent men, women, and children.

With the West African bishops, we call, in the words of the Fourth Assembly of the World Council of Churches held recently at Uppsala, for "all governments to work effectively towards peace and reconciliation, and to refrain from any action which would prolong the conflict in the area".

The Conference welcomes any agreement between the belligerent parties to provide channels for the supply of food, medicine, and clothing to those in need. It calls on governments to engage in a massive inter-governmental relief operation on both sides of the conflict, and commends the work of the Division of Inter-Church Aid, Refugee and World Service of the World Council of Churches and of other voluntary agencies in meeting immediate and longer-term needs.

The Conference assures its fellow Christians on both sides of the conflict of continuing fellowship with them in the gospel. They may be sure of the prayers of the bishops and Churches of the Anglican Communion and of all possible support, as in Christ's name they minister to the suffering and work for reconciliation and peace among all their people.

## The Middle East

15. The Conference views with concern the continuing tensions in the Middle East; the tragic plight of hundreds of thousands of Arab refugees who have lost homes and means of livelihood; and the absence, in spite of United Nations resolutions, of any sign of progress towards the establishment of peace. The Conference endorses the resolutions of the World Council of Churches at Uppsala and urges men of good will to use their influence in each nation and in the United Nations towards the finding of a just solution.

## Racism

16. The Conference commends the following statement of the World Council of Churches meeting at Uppsala:

> Racism is a blatant denial of the Christian faith. (1) It denies the effectiveness of the reconciling work of Jesus Christ, through whose love all human diversities lose their divisive significance; (2) it denies our common humanity in creation and our belief that all men are made in God's image ; (3) it falsely asserts that we find our significance in terms of racial identity rather than in Jesus Christ.

The Conference acknowledges in penitence that the Churches of the

Anglican Communion have failed to accept the cost of corporate witness to their unity in Christ, and calls upon them to re-examine their life and structures in order to give expression to the demands of the gospel (a) by the inclusiveness of their worship; (b) by the creation of a climate of acceptance in their common life; and (c) by their justice in placing and appointment.

Further, the Conference calls upon the Churches to press upon governments and communities their duty to promote fundamental human rights and freedoms among all their peoples.

The Conference welcomes especially the contribution of Human Rights Year towards the solution of the problem of racism.

## The Use of Power

17. The Conference, profoundly aware of the effect on human life of the responsible and irresponsible use of power at all levels of human society, considers that the Church should address itself energetically to the range of problems arising in this area.

## The Study of Social and Political Change

18. The Conference recommends that the provinces should set up study groups, Anglican and ecumenical, to study the documents on all aspects of violent and non-violent social and political change.

In view of the urgent nature of this matter, it further recommends that these groups promptly report their findings and recommendations to the Anglican Consultative Council or Lambeth Consultative Body, which will make them generally available to the Anglican Communion.

19. The Conference recommends:

(a) that, recognizing that for the foreseeable future the greater part of the earth will retain agrarian forms of society, the provinces of the Anglican Communion co-operate with the World Council of Churches and other agencies to carry out the regional surveys necessary to determine specific technological and other development needs in both agrarian and industrial areas;

and further, that the local Church in agrarian communities be urged to promote or co-operate in appropriate political, economic, and social development projects as its witness to the gospel of the incarnate Lord;

and that in both agrarian and industrial areas the structures of the Church, devised for static and pre-industrial societies, be renewed for more effective impact on rapidly changing societies.

(b) that the normal pattern for the missionary structure of the Church be that of ecumenical action and that every use be made of consultants from the social sciences and related fields.

(c) that the Church increasingly call on the skills of full-time professionals in such fields as social work, community organization, education, recreational activities, and the mass media, and that they be regarded as members of the integral staff of the Church.

(d) that the Church increasingly work for social goals which really benefit human beings, e.g. in housing, education, health, and adequate wages, using both secular agencies and, where appropriate, its own social agencies.

(e) that the Church increasingly give itself seriously to the redeployment of resources of men and money so as to take the initiatives that effective mission requires both at home and abroad.

(f) that, in consequence of the last recommendation, a serious study be made of existing buildings and the planning of new ones.

20. The Conference, conscious of the many and complex social, political, economic, and cultural problems of our time, on which Christians need guidance, urges upon the Anglican Communion the close study of the World Council of Churches Report *World Conference on Church and Society, 1966.*

*Developing Countries*

21. The Conference welcomes the deep concern about the economic and social frustration of developing countries expressed by the World Council of Churches at its recent Assembly in Uppsala. To produce decisive and wise action in this serious situation it recommends to the provinces of the Anglican Communion:

(a) the careful study of the issues of development including the new economic and political structures which it demands; and effective dissemination of knowledge about the issues to the Churches and to the public.

(b) that the efforts of the United Nations agencies to bring about world economic justice receive the active support and prayers of all the Churches.

(c) that they endorse the appeal of the World Council of Churches at Uppsala that the Churches should do their utmost to influence the governments of industrialized countries

(i) to increase annually the percentage of Gross National Product officially transferred as financial resources, exclusive of private investment, to developing countries, with the minimum net amount of one per cent to be reached by 1971;

(ii) to conclude agreements stabilizing and supporting at an acceptable level the prices of vulnerable primary products and providing preferential access to developed markets for the manufactured products of developing countries.

(d) that they should urge their members to support more actively existing funds, and particularly the Division of Inter-Church Aid, Refugee and World Service, to help meet some of the present emergencies in world poverty and hunger.

## Responsible Parenthood

22. This Conference has taken note of the papal encyclical letter *Humanae vitae* recently issued by His Holiness Pope Paul VI. The Conference records its appreciation of the Pope's deep concern for the institution of marriage and the integrity of married life.

Nevertheless, the Conference finds itself unable to agree with the Pope's conclusion that all methods of conception control other than abstinence from sexual intercourse or its confinement to the periods of infecundity are contrary to the "order established by God". It reaffirms the findings of the Lambeth Conference of 1958 contained in resolutions 112, 113, and 115 which are as follows:

112. The Conference records its profound conviction that the idea of the human family is rooted in the Godhead and that consequently all problems of sex relations, the procreation of children, and the organization of family life must be related, consciously and directly, to the creative, redemptive, and sanctifying power of God.

113. The Conference affirms that marriage is a vocation to holiness, through which men and women may share in the love and creative purpose of God. The sins of self-indulgence and sensuality, born of selfishness and a refusal to accept marriage as a divine vocation, destroy its true nature and depth and the right fullness and balance of the relationship between men and women. Christians need always to remember that sexual love is not an end in itself nor a means to self-gratification, and that self-discipline and restraint are essential conditions of the responsible freedom of marriage and family planning.

115. The Conference believes that the responsibility for deciding upon the number and frequency of children has been laid by God upon the consciences of parents everywhere: that this planning, in such ways as are mutually acceptable to husband and wife in Christian conscience, is a right and important factor in Christian family life and should be the result of positive choice before God. Such responsible parenthood, built on obedience to all the duties of marriage, requires a wise stewardship of the resources and abilities of the family as well as a thoughtful consideration of the varying population needs and problems of society and the claims of future generations.

The Conference commends the report of Committee 5 of the Lambeth Conference 1958, together with the study entitled *The Family in Contemporary Society* which formed the basis of the work of that Committee, to the attention of all men of good will for further study in the light of the continuing sociological and scientific developments of the past decade.

### Marriage Discipline

23. The Conference recognizes that polygamy poses one of the sharpest conflicts between the faith and particular cultures.

The Church seeks to proclaim the will of God in setting out the clear implications of our Lord's teaching about marriage. Hence it bears witness to monogamous lifelong marriage as God's will for mankind.

The Conference believes that such marriage alone bears adequate witness to the equal sanctity of all human beings which lies at the heart of the Christian revelation; yet recognizes that in every place many problems concerning marriage confront the Church.

The Conference therefore asks each province to re-examine its discipline in such problems in full consultation with other provinces in a similar situation.

### THE MINISTRY (*Resolutions 24-41*)

### The Laity

24. The Conference recommends that no major issue in the life of the Church should be decided without the full participation of the laity in discussion and in decision.

25. The Conference recommends that each province or regional Church be asked to explore the theology of baptism and confirmation in relation to the need to commission the laity for their task in the world, and to experiment in this regard.

26.   The Conference requests that information about experiments in lay training be made available to the whole of the Anglican Communion.

27.   The Conference believes that there is an urgent need for increase in the quantity and quality of training available for laypeople for their task in the world.

*Youth and Human Welfare*

28.   The Conference values the initiative shown by young people in witnessing to their faith in Christ; and urges that they should be encouraged to do this in their own way and through their own media, and that the Church should have regard to their concern for the renewal of society and of the Church.

29.   The Conference, thankful for the intensified interest of young people in human welfare, conscious of the value of their informed insights, and recognizing the need to involve them more directly in decision-making, in both secular and ecclesiastical society, requests provinces, dioceses, and parishes to promote this involvement in every way possible.

*Fellowships for Church Women*

30.   The Conference welcomes the appearance of Fellowships for Church Women in various parts of the Anglican Communion and commends the development and extension of these associations for an increase of devotion and neighbourliness and for witness to the faith of Jesus Christ.

*Priesthood*

31.   The Conference commends the study of the paragraphs on "Priesthood" in the report of Section II as an Anglican contribution towards an understanding of the nature of priesthood in the present ecumenical situation.

*The Diaconate*

32.   The Conference recommends:

(*a*) That the diaconate, combining service of others with liturgical functions, be open to
(i) men and women remaining in secular occupations
(ii) full-time church workers
(iii) those selected for the priesthood.

(b) That Ordinals should, where necessary, be revised:

(i) to take account of the new role envisaged for the diaconate;

(ii) by the removal of reference to the diaconate as "an inferior office";

(iii) by emphasis upon the continuing element of *diakonia* in the ministry of bishops and priests.

(c) That those made deaconesses by laying on of hands with appropriate prayers be declared to be within the diaconate. (*For*, 221. *Against*, 183.)

(d) That appropriate canonical legislation be enacted by provinces and regional Churches to provide for those already ordained deaconesses.

## A Wider Ordained Ministry

33. This Conference reaffirms Resolution 89 of the Lambeth Conference 1958 on the Supplementary Ministry and recommends a wider and more confident use of this ministry. The Resolution reads as follows:

89. The Conference considers that, while the fully-trained and full-time priesthood is essential to the continuing life of the Church, there is no theological principle which forbids a suitable man from being ordained priest while continuing in his lay occupation. While calling attention to Resolution 65 of the Lambeth Conference of 1930, the Conference now wishes to go further and to encourage provinces to make provision on these lines in cases where conditions make it desirable. Such provision is not to be regarded as a substitute for the full-time ministry of the Church, but as an addition to it.

## Ordination of Women to the Priesthood

34. The Conference affirms its opinion that the theological arguments as at present presented for and against the ordination of women to the priesthood are inconclusive.

35. The Conference requests every national and regional Church or province to give careful study to the question of the ordination of women to the priesthood and to report its findings to the Anglican Consultative Council (or Lambeth Consultative Body) which will make them generally available to the Anglican Communion.

36.  The Conference requests the Anglican Consultative Council (or Lambeth Consultative Body)

(*a*) to initiate consultations with other Churches which have women in their ordained ministry and with those which have not.

(*b*) to distribute the information thus secured throughout the Anglican Communion.

37.  The Conference recommends that, before any national or regional Church or province makes a final decision to ordain women to the priesthood, the advice of the Anglican Consulative Council (or Lambeth Consultative Body) be sought and carefully considered.

38.  The Conference recommends that, in the meantime, national or regional Churches or provinces should be encouraged to make canonical provision, where this does not exist, for duly qualified women to share in the conduct of liturgical worship, to preach, to baptize, to read the epistle and gospel at the Holy Communion, and to help in the distribution of the elements.

*The Episcopate*

39.  The Conference recommends that bishops should have opportunities of training for their office and requests the Anglican Consultative Council to make provision for such training where regional Churches are unable to do so.

40.  The Conference affirms its opinion that all coadjutor, suffragan, and full-time assistant bishops should exercise every kind of episcopal function and have their place as bishops in the councils of the Church.

41.  The Conference recommends that the bishops, as leaders and representatives of a servant Church, should radically examine the honours paid to them in the course of divine worship, in titles and customary address, and in style of living, while having the necessary facilities for the efficient carrying on of their work.

*Post-Ordination Training*

42.  The Conference urges dioceses to provide continuing training for the clergy after ordination, and to relate the programmes of study to the new situations and developments presented by a rapidly changing world.

*The Thirty-nine Articles*

43.  The Conference accepts the main conclusion of the report of the Archbishops' Commission on Christian Doctrine entitled *Subscription*

*and Assent to the Thirty-nine Articles* (1968) and in furtherance of its recommendation

- (*a*) suggests that each Church of our communion consider whether the Articles need be bound up with its Prayer Book;

- (*b*) suggests to the Churches of the Anglican Communion that assent to the Thirty-nine Articles be no longer required of ordinands.

- (*c*) suggests that, when subscription is required to the Articles or other elements in the Anglican tradition, it should be required, and given, only in the context of a statement which gives the full range of our inheritance of faith and sets the Articles in their historical context.

(37 *dissentients.*)

RELATIONS WITH OTHER CHURCHES (*Resolutions 44–59*)

*Renewal in Unity*

44. The Conference recommends that the following affirmations be referred to each province for consideration, as means of furthering renewal in unity.

(*a*) We believe that each bishop of the Anglican Communion should ask himself how seriously he takes the suggestion of the Lund Conference on Faith and Order that we should do together everything which conscience does not compel us to do separately. To do so immediately raises the need to review church structures (conduct of synods, budgets, areas of jurisdiction, etc.) to see where they can be altered to foster rather than hinder co-operation. It involves giving encouragement in this direction to all whom we can influence. It involves also the exploration of *responsible experiment* so that ecumenical work beyond the present limits of constitutional provision is encouraged to keep in touch with the common mind of the Church and not tempted to break away.

(*b*) We believe that prior attention in ecumenical life and action should be given to the local level, and point to local ecumenical action as the most direct way of bringing together the whole Christian community in any area.

(*c*) We believe that as ecumenical work develops in local, national, and regional areas the need becomes more apparent for an ecumenical forum on the widest possible scale. We therefore endorse the hope expressed at the Uppsala Assembly that "the members of the World Council of Churches, committed to each other, should work for the time when a genuinely universal council may once more speak for all

Christians".. Our interim confessional and ecumenical organizations should be tested by their capacity to lead in this direction.

(d) We believe that areas in which little ecumenical activity is at present possible have a claim upon the encouragement and support of the more strongly established areas, which should make provision of time and money to maintain fellowship with them.

## Admission of Non-Anglicans to Holy Communion

45. The Conference recommends that, in order to meet special pastoral needs of God's people, under the direction of the bishop Christians duly baptized in the name of the Holy Trinity and qualified to receive Holy Communion in their own Churches may be welcomed at the Lord's table in the Anglican Communion.

## Anglicans Communicating in other than Anglican Churches

46. The Conference recommends that, while it is the general practice of the Church that Anglican communicants receive the Holy Communion at the hands of ordained ministers of their own Church or of Churches in communion therewith, nevertheless under the general direction of the bishop, to meet special pastoral need, such communicants be free to attend the Eucharist in other Churches holding the apostolic faith as contained in the Scriptures and summarized in the Apostles' and Nicene Creeds, and as conscience dictates to receive the sacrament, when they know they are welcome to do so. (For, 351. Against, 75.)

## Reciprocal Acts of Intercommunion

47. The Conference recommends that, where there is agreement between an Anglican Church and some other Church or Churches to seek unity in a way which includes agreement on apostolic faith and order, and where that agreement to seek unity has found expression, whether in a covenant to unite or in some other appropriate form, a Church of the Anglican Communion should be free to allow reciprocal acts of intercommunion under the general direction of the bishop; each province concerned to determine when the negotiations for union in which it is engaged have reached the stage which allows this intercommunion. (For, 341. Against, 87.)

## The Church of South India

48. The Conference recommends:

(a) that when a bishop or episcopally ordained minister of the Church of South India visits a diocese of the Anglican Communion and exercises his ministry in Anglican churches there should now be no restriction on the exercise of his ministry in other Churches with which the Church of South India is in communion.

(b) that Churches and Provinces of the Anglican Communion re-examine their relation to the Church of South India with a view to entering into full communion with that Church.

## The Churches of North India and Pakistan

49. The Conference recommends that Churches and provinces of the Anglican Communion should enter into full communion with the Churches of North India and Pakistan upon their inauguration and should foster the relations of fellowship which this involves.

## The Church of Lanka

50. The Conference recommends that Churches and provinces of the Anglican Communion should enter into full communion with the Church of Lanka upon its inauguration and should foster the relations of fellowship which this involves.

## Anglican–Methodist Unity in Great Britain

51. The Conference welcomes the proposals for Anglican–Methodist unity in Great Britain and notes with satisfaction the view expressed in the report of Section III that the proposed Service of Reconciliation is theologically adequate to achieve its declared intentions of reconciling the two Churches and integrating their ministries.

## The Roman Catholic Church

52. The Conference welcomes the proposals made in the report of Section III which concern Anglican relations with the Roman Catholic Church.

53. The Conference recommends the setting up of a Permanent Joint Commission, for which the Anglican delegation should be chosen by the Lambeth Consultative Body (or its successor) and be representative of the Anglican Communion as a whole.

54. In view of the urgent pastoral questions raised by mixed marriages the Conference welcomes the work of the Joint Commission on the Theology of Marriage and its Application to Mixed Marriages, and urges its speedy continuance.

*Collegiality*

55. The Conference recommends that the principle of collegiality should be a guiding principle in the growth of the relationships between the provinces of the Anglican Communion and those Churches with which we are, or shall be, in full communion, and draws particular attention to that part of the Section III report which underlines this principle.

*The Orthodox Churches*

56. The Conference warmly welcomes the proposed resumption of the pan-Orthodox and pan-Anglican discussions which began in 1931.

57. The Conference welcomes the proposals concerning Anglican relations with the Orthodox and Oriental (Orthodox) Churches, urging joint biblical study with Orthodox theologians and dialogue at the local level.

58. The Conference recommends the circulation to all Anglican provinces of the report of the delegation to Bucharest in 1935 and of the terms in which this report was accepted and endorsed by the Convocations of Canterbury and York "as consonant with the Anglican formularies and a legitimate interpretation of the faith of the Church as held by the Anglican Communion".

*The Lutheran Churches*

59. The Conference recommends the initiation of Anglican–Lutheran conversations on a worldwide basis as soon as possible.

THE ROLE OF THE ANGLICAN COMMUNION (*Resolutions 60–69*)

*The Anglican Presence in Europe*

60. The Conference welcomes the proposals in the report of Section III concerning the Anglican presence in Europe.

*The Anglican Centre in Rome*

61. The Conference expresses its willingness to support the Anglican Centre in Rome, which with its library and its facilities for lectures, discussions, and personal advice, will help Roman Catholics and others to learn more about the life and thought of the Anglican Communion in all its aspects.

*The Anglican Presence in Geneva*

62. The Conference recommends that the Anglican presence in Geneva should be strengthened, and that the Lambeth Consultative Body (or its successor) should take appropriate steps to effect this.

*Parallel Jurisdictions*

63. The Conference deplores the existence of parallel Anglican jurisdictions in Europe and in other areas, and recommends that the Lambeth Consultative Body (or its successor) should give early attention to the problems involved. The Conference recommends that, in any such area where there exists a Church with which we are in full communion, that Church should participate in the consultations.

*The Anglican Presence in Latin America*

64. The Conference records its conviction that, in the light of the growing importance of Latin America and the rapid social, economic, political, and religious changes there taking place, there is an urgent need for an increasing Christian witness and involvement in which the Anglican Churches must make their unique and full contribution.

The Conference rejoices in the growth and indigenization of Anglican witness in Latin America since Lambeth 1958 and in the increased participation and awareness of some parts of the Anglican Communion, and hopes that this participation and interest will extend to the whole Anglican Communion.

The Conference recommends that the member Churches of the Anglican Communion should place prominent emphasis upon Latin America in their missionary education, their prayers, and their commitment to the world mission, as outlined in the document entitled *The Anglican Communion and Latin America.*

*General Episcopal Consultation*

65. The Conference recommends:

(a) that a General Episcopal Consultation (drawn from many countries) be held in the near future, and expresses the hope that the Archbishop of Canterbury will take the initiative in sending invitations primarily to those Churches which are in full or partial communion with the see of Canterbury or with other provinces of the Anglican Communion.

(b) that Regional Episcopal Consultations should be held on a wider basis of representation than that suggested for the General Episcopal Consultation, under such local auspices and arrangements as seem appropriate and helpful in each region.

*Inter-Anglican Structures*

66. The Conference approves the recommendations listed under the general heading Inter-Anglican Structures in the report of Section III.

*Mutual Responsibility and Interdependence*

67. (*a*) The Conference records its gratitude for the concept of Mutual Responsibility and Interdependence in the Body of Christ, and for the renewed sense of responsibility for each other which it has created within our communion.

(*b*) The Conference believes that a developing M.R.I. has a vital contribution to make to our relationships within the whole Church of God. It therefore summons our Churches to a deeper commitment to Christ's mission through a wide partnership of prayer, by sharing sacrificially and effectively their manpower and money, and by a readiness to learn from each other.

(*c*) The Conference urges that serious attention be paid to the need for co-operation, at every level of Anglican and ecumenical life, in the planning, implementing, and review of all work undertaken, along the lines set out in the report of Section III (para. 6 on p. 146).

(*d*) The Conference believes that the time has come for a reappraisal of the policies, methods, and areas of responsibility of the Anglican Communion in discharging its share of the mission of Christ and that there is a need for a renewed sense of urgency.

*Budgets*

68. The Conference approves the approximate budgets for 1969, 1970, and 1971 submitted by the *ad hoc* finance committee and asks the member Churches to support this Central Budget according to the present tables of apportionment.

*Anglican Consultative Council*

69. The Conference accepts and endorses the appended proposals concerning the Anglican Consultative Council and its Constitution and submits them to the member Churches of the Anglican Communion for approval. Approval shall be by a two-thirds majority of the member Churches and shall be signified to the Secretary of the Lambeth Consultative Body not later than 31 October 1969.

## ANGLICAN CONSULTATIVE COUNCIL

FUNCTIONS

1. To share information about developments in one or more provinces with the other parts of the communion and to serve as needed as an instrument of common action.

2. To advise on inter-Anglican, provincial, and diocesan relationships, including the division of provinces, the formation of new provinces and of regional councils, and the problems of extra-provincial dioceses.

3. To develop as far as possible agreed Anglican policies in the world mission of the Church and to encourage national and regional Churches to engage together in developing and implementing such policies by sharing their resources of manpower, money, and experience to the best advantage of all.

4. To keep before national and regional Churches the importance of the fullest possible Anglican collaboration with other Christian Churches.

5. To encourage and guide Anglican participation in the Ecumenical Movement and the ecumenical organizations; to co-operate with the World Council of Churches and the world confessional bodies on behalf of the Anglican Communion; and to make arrangements for the conduct of pan-Anglican conversations with the Roman Catholic Church, the Orthodox Churches, and other Churches.

6. To advise on matters arising out of national or regional church union negotiations or conversations and on subsequent relations with united Churches.

7. To advise on problems of inter-Anglican communication and to help in the dissemination of Anglican and ecumenical information.

8. To keep in review the needs that may arise for further study and, where necessary, to promote inquiry and research.

CONSTITUTION

*Membership*

1. The Council shall be constituted initially with a membership according to the Schedule below. With the assent of two-thirds of the Metropolitans, it shall have power to make alterations in the Schedule as changing circumstances may require.

2. Members shall be chosen as provincial, national, or regional machinery provides. Alternates shall be named by each Church and shall be invited to attend if a Church would otherwise be unrepresented for a whole session of the council.

3. The Council shall have power to co-opt as set out in the Schedule of Membership.

4. The term of office for members appointed according to the Schedule, and for co-opted members, shall be six years. Except as provided in the recommendation below for the initial period,

members shall be ineligible for immediate re-election. Bishops and other clerical members shall cease to be members on retirement from ecclesiastical office, and all members shall similarly cease to be members on moving to another regional Church or province of the Anglican Communion. Casual vacancies shall be filled by the appointing bodies, and persons thus appointed shall serve for the unexpired term.

5. The Council shall have the right to call in advisers, Anglicans or others, at its discretion.

6. *Officers*

    (a) The Archbishop of Canterbury shall be President of the Council and, when present, shall preside at the inaugural session of each meeting of the Council. He shall be *ex officio* a member of its committees.

    (b) The Council shall elect a Chairman and Vice-Chairman from its own number, who shall hold office for six years.

    (c) The Council shall appoint for a specified term a Secretary, who shall be known as the Secretary General of the Council, and shall determine his duties.

7. *Frequency of Meetings*

    The Council shall meet every two years at the call of the Chairman in consultation with the President and the Secretary General.

8. *Standing Committee*

    The Council shall appoint a Standing Committee of nine members, which shall include the Chairman and Vice-Chairman of the Council. The Secretary General shall be its Secretary. The Standing Committee shall meet annually. It shall have the right to call advisers.

9. *Locality of Meetings*

    As far as possible, the Council and its Standing Committee shall meet in various parts of the world.

10. *Budget*

    The Council shall produce an annual budget, including the stipend and expenses of the Secretary General, his staff, and office, and this shall be apportioned among the member Churches of the Anglican Communion.

11. *Amendment of the Constitution*

    Amendments to this Constitution shall be submitted by the Council to the constitutional bodies of the member Churches and must be ratified by two-thirds of such bodies.

N.B. It is recommended that, in order to provide for continuity in Council membership, at the beginning one-third of the delegates shall be appointed as elected for a two-year period, one-third for a four-year period, and the remaining third for a single period of six years. Those elected for a two-year or four-year period shall be eligible for appointment for one further period of six years. Thereafter all appointments or elections shall be for six years.

## Schedule of Membership

The membership of the Council shall be as follows:

(a) The Archbishop of Canterbury

(b) Three from each of the following, consisting of a bishop, a priest or deacon, and a lay person:

> The Church of England
> The Episcopal Church in the United States of America
> The Church of India, Pakistan, Burma, and Ceylon
> The Anglican Church of Canada
> The Church of England in Australia.

(c) Two from each of the following, consisting of a bishop, and a priest, deacon, or lay person:

> The Church in Wales
> The Church of Ireland
> The Episcopal Church in Scotland
> The Church of the Province of South Africa
> The Church of the Province of West Africa
> The Church of the Province of Central Africa
> The Church of the Province of East Africa
> The Church of the Province of Uganda, Rwanda, and Burundi
> The Church of the Province of New Zealand
> The Church of the Province of the West Indies
> Nippon Sei Ko Kai
> The Archbishopric in Jerusalem
> The Council of the Church of South-East Asia
> The South Pacific Anglican Council
> Latin America.
> any Province of the Anglican Communion not at present represented.

(d) Co-opted members. The Council shall have power to co-opt up to six additional members, of whom at least two shall be women and two lay persons not over 28 years of age at the time of appointment.

## STATEMENT FROM THE
## BISHOPS OF THE PROVINCE OF WEST AFRICA

*Referred to in Resolution 14*

The Bishops of the Province of West Africa desire to give thanks to Almighty God for the prayers, the sympathy, and the work for reconciliation which have supported us and have enabled us to endure these fourteen months of civil war. We are especially grateful to His Grace the Archbishop of Canterbury for his message sent to us when war broke out, for his initiative in the visits of fraternal delegations to the churches on both sides, and for his persistent work for peace. We were heartened by the joint appeal for peace made in March by the Roman Catholic Church and the World Council of Churches, calling for "an immediate cessation of armed hostilities and for the establishment of a lasting peace by honourable negotiation in the highest African tradition". We are grateful to the Commonwealth Secretariat and to the Organization of African Unity for the efforts they have made and are continuing to make to bring the two sides together. We also desire to record our deep gratitude to the voluntary agencies and to our fellow Christians in all parts of the world who have contributed by their generous gifts, their prayers, and their concern to alleviate the sufferings of our war-saddened peoples.

Yet the war still goes on. We are deeply grieved and feel bound to acknowledge in penitence our ineffective witness to the compassion and mercy and reconciling love of Christ. In our failure we seek the sympathetic aid of the Lambeth Conference in action as follows:

1. To call, in the words of the Resolution of the Uppsala World Council meeting, for "all governments to work effectively towards peace and reconciliation, and to refrain from any action which would prolong the conflict in the area".

2. To call on the government of both sides in the war to look with pity on those who are sick and starving and to give every facility to the organizations which are endeavouring to bring them food and medical supplies.

3. To consider offering, in co-operation with other Churches, a further delegation to visit the leaders on both sides to promote the work of reconciliation so powerfully put before us in the Archbishop of East Africa's sermon.

Finally, we state our belief that the conflict can be resolved positively in a creative way only when each side is prepared to abandon exclusive positions and to seek to reach agreement on how to secure the vital interests of the peoples of both sides.

## NOTE

The following Reports must be taken as having the authority only of the Sections by which they were respectively prepared and presented.

The Conference as a whole is responsible only for the formal Resolutions agreed to after discussion and printed on pp. 27–49 of this volume.

# ABBREVIATIONS

| | |
|---|---|
| E | The Church of England |
| W | The Church in Wales |
| I | The Church of Ireland |
| S | The Episcopal Church in Scotland |
| US | The Protestant Episcopal Church in the United States of America |
| Can | The Anglican Church of Canada |
| IPBC | The Church of India, Pakistan, Burma, and Ceylon |
| Aus | The Church of England in Australia |
| NZ | The Church of the Province of New Zealand |
| SA | The Church of the Province of South Africa |
| WI | The Church in the Province of the West Indies |
| NSKK | Nippon Sei Ko Kai |
| CHSKH | Chung Hua Sheng Kung Hui (represented by the Bishop of Hong Kong) |
| WA | The Church of the Province of West Africa |
| CA | The Church of the Province of Central Africa |
| Jer | The Archbishopric in Jerusalem |
| EA | The Church of the Province of East Africa |
| Ug | The Church of Uganda, Rwanda, and Burundi |
| Brazil | Igreja Episcopal do Brasil |
| XP | Extra-Provincial Dioceses under the jurisdiction of the Archbishop of Canterbury are shown at the end of the list in every case. Extra-provincial dioceses under the jurisdiction of PECUSA or the Church in Australia are shown in the appropriate place. |
| XPX | Iglesia Episcopal de Cuba |

# REPORT OF SECTION I
The Renewal of the Church in Faith

## SECTION OFFICERS

| | |
|---|---|
| The Primate of Canada | H. H. Clark (Chairman) |
| The Bishop of Durham | I. T. Ramsey (Vice-Chairman) |
| The Archbishop of Wales | W. G. H. Simon (Secretary) |

## (a) THE LANGUAGE OF FAITH

### SUBCOMMITTEE 1

### THE NATURE OF THEOLOGICAL LANGUAGE

| | | |
|---|---|---|
| E | Bishop of Birmingham | J. L. Wilson (Vice-Chairman) |
| | Bishop of Manchester | W. D. L. Greer |
| | Bishop Suffragan of Huntingdon (Ely) | R. A. S. Martineau |
| | Assistant Bishop of Rochester | J. K. Russell |
| US | Bishop of Alabama | C. C. J. Carpenter |
| | Bishop of Long Island | J. G. Sherman |
| | Bishop of Northern Indiana | W. C. Klein |
| | Bishop of South Florida | H. I. Louttit |
| | Bishop Suffragan of Mexico | M. Saucedo |
| Can | Bishop of Ontario | K. C. Evans (Chairman) |
| Aus | Bishop of Gippsland | D. A. Garnsey (Secretary) |

### SUBCOMMITTEE 2

### THE DEBATE ABOUT GOD

| | | |
|---|---|---|
| E | Bishop of Bradford | C. G. St M. Parker |
| | Bishop of Leicester | R. R. Williams |
| | Assistant Bishop of Sheffield | G. V. Gerard |
| S | Bishop of St Andrews, | J. W. A. Howe (Secretary) |
| | Dunkeld and Dunblane | |
| US | Bishop of East Carolina | T. H. Wright |
| | Bishop of Lexington | W. R. Moody |
| | Bishop of Missouri | G. L. Cadigan |
| | Bishop of North Dakota | G. T. Masuda |
| | Bishop of Panama and the Canal Zone | R. H. Gooden |
| | Bishop of Springfield | A. A. Chambers |
| | Bishop of Washington | W. F. Creighton (Vice-Chairman) |
| | Bishop Suffragan of Long Island | R. B. Martin |
| Can | Bishop of Saskatoon | S. C. Steer (Chairman) |
| Aus | Archbishop of Sydney | M. L. Loane |
| SA | Bishop Suffragan of Lesotho | F. Makhetha |
| WA | Bishop of Ekiti | M. A. Osanyin |

## SUBCOMMITTEE 3
## THE FINALITY OF CHRIST

| | | |
|---|---|---|
| E | Bishop of St Edmundsbury and Ipswich | L. W. Brown (Chairman) |
| | Bishop Suffragan of Bedford (St Albans) | J. T. H. Hare |
| | Bishop Suffragan of Sherborne (Salisbury) | V. J. Pike |
| US | Bishop of Atlanta | R. R. Claiborne Jr |
| | Bishop of Dallas | C. A. Mason |
| | Bishop of Kentucky | C. G. Marmion |
| Can | Archbishop of Fredericton | A. H. O'Neil |
| | Bishop of Keewatin | H. E. Hives |
| | Bishop Suffragan of Nova Scotia | G. F. Arnold |
| IPBC | Bishop of Karachi | C. Ray (Vice-Chairman) |
| Aus | Bishop of Canberra and Goulburn | K. J. Clements |
| SA | Bishop of Lesotho | J. A. A. Maund |
| | General Secretary of the Christian Council of South Africa | B. B. Burnett (Secretary) |
| WA | Assistant Bishop on the Niger | L. M. Uzodike |
| XP | Bishop of Mauritius | E. E. Curtis |

## SUBCOMMITTEE 4
## DIALOGUE WITH OTHER FAITHS

| | | |
|---|---|---|
| E | Bishop Suffragan of Crediton (Exeter) | W. A. E. Westall |
| W | Bishop of St Davids | J. R. Richards |
| US | Bishop of Northern California | C. R. Haden Jr (Vice-Chairman) |
| | Bishop of Texas | J. M. Richardson |
| | Bishop of Utah | R. S. Watson |
| Can | Bishop of Niagara | W. E. Bagnall |
| IPBC | Bishop of Andaman and Nicobar Islands | M. D. Srinivasan |
| Aus | Archbishop of Perth | G. Appleton (Chairman) |
| Jer | Bishop in Iran | H. B. Dehqani-Tafti (Secretary) |
| | Bishop in the Sudan | O. C. Allison |
| EA | Bishop of Victoria Nyanza | M. L. Wiggins |
| Ug | Bishop of Northern Uganda | S. G. Wani |

## SUBCOMMITTEE 5
### THE VARIETIES OF UNBELIEF

| | | |
|---|---|---|
| E | Bishop of Wakefield | E. Treacy |
| | Bishop Suffragan of Dorchester (Oxford) | D. G. Loveday |
| | Bishop Suffragan of Hulme (Manchester) | K. V. Ramsey |
| | Bishop Suffragan of Taunton (Bath and Wells) | F. H. West (Vice-Chairman) |
| W | Bishop of Bangor | G. O. Williams (Secretary) |
| US | Bishop Suffragan of Northern California | E. McNair |
| | Bishop Suffragan of Texas | S. F. Bailey |
| Can | Bishop of Yukon | J. T. Frame |
| | Bishop Suffragan of Newfoundland | W. G. Legge |
| WA | Bishop of Sierra Leone | M. N. C. O. Scott |
| EA | Bishop of Masasi | E. U. T. Huddleston (Chairman) |
| | Bishop of Western Tanganyika | M. Kahurananga |

## SUBCOMMITTEE 6
### CONFESSING THE FAITH TODAY

| | | |
|---|---|---|
| E | Bishop of Salisbury | J. E. Fison (Secretary) |
| | Bishop of Blackburn | C. R. Claxton |
| | Bishop Suffragan of Woolwich (Southwark) | J. A. T. Robinson |
| | Assistant Bishop of Chichester | R. A. Reeves |
| | Assistant Bishop of Derby | T. R. Parfitt |
| I | Bishop of Ossory, Ferns, and Leighlin | H. R. McAdoo (Chairman) |
| S | Bishop of Moray, Ross, and Caithness | D. Macinnes |
| US | Bishop of Albany | A. W. Brown |
| | Bishop of Oklahoma | C. Powell (Vice-Chairman) |
| | Bishop Suffragan of Dallas | W. P. Barnds |
| | Bishop Suffragan of New Jersey | A. W. Van Duzer |
| Can | Bishop of the Arctic | D. B. Marsh |
| Aus | Bishop of Armidale | R. C. Kerle |
| NZ | Archbishop of New Zealand | N. A. Lesser |
| XP | Bishop of Argentina and Eastern South America with the Falkland Islands | C. J. Tucker |
| XPX | Bishop of Cuba | J. A. Gonzalez |

## (b) THE EXPERIENCE OF FAITH

SUBCOMMITTEE 7

THE PSYCHOLOGY OF FAITH

| | | |
|---|---|---|
| E | Bishop Suffragan of Stafford (Lichfield) | R. G. Clitherow |
| I | Bishop of Kilmore and Elphin and Ardagh | E. F. B. Moore |
| S | Bishop of Edinburgh | K. M. Carey (Chairman) |
| US | Bishop of Easton | G. A. Taylor |
| | Bishop of Pittsburgh | A. Pardue |
| | Bishop Suffragan of Texas | F. P. Goddard |
| | Assistant Bishop of South Florida | A. E. Swift (Secretary) |
| Can | Bishop of Caledonia | E. G. Munn |
| SA | Bishop of Kimberley and Kuruman | P. W. Wheeldon |
| WI | Archbishop of the West Indies | A. J. Knight |
| Ug | Archbishop of Uganda, Rwanda, and Burundi | E. Sabiti (Vice-Chairman) |

SUBCOMMITTEE 8

FAITH AND SOCIETY

| | | |
|---|---|---|
| E | Bishop of Peterborough | C. Eastaugh |
| US | Presiding Bishop of the Protestant Episcopal Church in the United States of America | J. E. Hines |
| | Bishop of Florida | E. H. West |
| | Bishop of Southwestern Virginia | W. H. Marmion |
| | Bishop of Wyoming | J. W. Hunter |
| Can | Bishop of Brandon | I. A. Norris |
| IPBC | Bishop of Lucknow | J. Amritanand |
| Aus | Bishop Coadjutor of Melbourne | G. T. Sambell (Secretary) |
| NZ | Bishop of Auckland | E. A. Gowing (Chairman) |
| | Bishop Suffragan in Polynesia | F. T. Halapua |
| WI | Bishop of Trinidad and Tobago | W. J. Hughes |
| CA | Bishop of Mashonaland | J. P. Burrough |
| Jer | Assistant Bishop in the Sudan | E. J. Ngalamu |
| Ug | Bishop of Ankole | K. Shalita |
| | Bishop of Namirembe | D. K. Nsubuga (Vice-Chairman) |
| Brazil | Primate of the Episcopal Church of Brazil | E. M. Krischke |

## SUBCOMMITTEE 9
## SPIRITUALITY AND FAITH

| | | |
|---|---|---|
| E | Bishop Suffragan of Barking (Chelmsford) | W. F. P. Chadwick (Chairman) |
| | Bishop Suffragan of Jarrow (Durham) | A. K. Hamilton |
| | Bishop Suffragan of Lancaster (Blackburn) | A. L. E. Hoskyns-Abrahall |
| | Bishop Suffragan of Plymouth (Exeter) | W. G. Sanderson |
| S | Bishop of Brechin | J. C. Sprott |
| US | Bishop of Maryland | H. L. Doll |
| | Bishop of West Virginia | W. C. Campbell |
| Can | Bishop Suffragan of St Clair (Huron) | C. J. Queen |
| IPBC | Bishop of Amritsar | E. S. Nasir (Secretary) |
| Aus | Archbishop of Brisbane | P. N. W. Strong |
| | Bishop of Riverina | J. B. R. Grindrod |
| EA | Bishop of Maseno | F. H. Olang' (Vice-Chairman) |
| | Assistant Bishop of Central Tanganyika | Y. Madinda |
| Ug | Assistant Bishop of Ruwenzori | Y. Rwakaikara |
| XP | Bishop of Bermuda | J. Armstrong |

## SUBCOMMITTEE 10
## FAITH AND CULTURE

| | | |
|---|---|---|
| E | Bishop of Norwich | W. L. S. Fleming (Chairman) |
| US | Bishop of South Carolina | G. Temple |
| | Bishop of Spokane | J. R. Wyatt |
| | Bishop of the Virgin Islands | C. E. Mills |
| | Bishop Coadjutor of Minnesota | P. F. McNairy |
| | Bishop Suffragan of South Florida | W. L. Hargrave |
| | Bishop Suffragan of Tennessee | W. F. Gates Jr |
| | Director, Home Department of PECUSA | D. Corrigan |
| Can | Bishop of Moosonee | J. A. Watton |
| | Bishop Coadjutor of Rupert's Land | J. O. Anderson |
| IPBC | Bishop of Kurunagala | C. L. Wickremesinghe (Vice-Chairman) |
| Aus | Bishop of Carpentaria | E. E. Hawkey |
| NZ | Bishop of Melanesia | J. W. Chisholm |
| SA | Bishop of George | P. H. F. Barron |
| WA | Assistant Bishop of Accra | J. B. Arthur |
| Ug | Bishop of West Buganda | S. S. Tomusange |
| XP | Bishop of Taejon | C. R. Rutt (Secretary) |

## (c) THE FAITH AND SECULAR SOCIETY

SUBCOMMITTEE 11

CHRISTIAN APPRAISAL OF THE SECULAR SOCIETY

| | | |
|---|---|---|
| E | Bishop of Lincoln | K. Riches |
| | Bishop of Newcastle (U.K.) | H. E. Ashdown |
| | Bishop Suffragan of Tewkesbury (Gloucester) | F. T. Horan |
| | Bishop Suffragan of Thetford (Norwich) | E. W. B. Cordingly |
| | Assistant Bishop of Bath and Wells | D. J. Wilson |
| US | Bishop of Los Angeles | F. E. I. Bloy |
| | Bishop of Ohio | J. H. Burt |
| | Bishop of Puerto Rico | F. Reus-Froylan |
| Can | Bishop of Kootenay | E. W. Scott |
| | Bishop of Ottawa | E. S. Reed (Chairman) |
| WI | Bishop Suffragan of Trinidad and Tobago (in Venezuela) | G. Marshall |
| CA | Bishop of Matabeleland | K. J. F. Skelton (Secretary) |
| Jer | Bishop in Jordan, Lebanon, and Syria | N. A. Cuba'in |
| EA | Bishop of Dar-es-Salaam | J. Sepeku (Vice-Chairman) |

SUBCOMMITTEE 12

INTERNATIONAL MORALITY TODAY

| | | |
|---|---|---|
| E | Bishop of Chichester | R. P. Wilson (Chairman) |
| I | Bishop of Killaloe, Kilfenora, Clonfert, and Kilmacduagh | H. A. Stanistreet |
| US | Bishop of Alaska | W. J. Gordon Jr |
| | Bishop of Vermont | H. D. Butterfield |
| | Bishop Suffragan of Albany | C. B. Persell Jr |
| Can | Bishop of Toronto | G. B. Snell (Secretary) |
| Aus | Bishop of Kalgoorlie | D. W. Bryant |
| | Bishop of the Northern Territory | K. B. Mason |
| NZ | Bishop of Waikato | J. T. Holland |
| SA | Bishop of Damaraland | R. H. Mize |
| CHSKH | Bishop of Hong Kong and Macao | J. G. H. Baker (Vice-Chairman) |
| WA | Bishop of Ondo | I. O. S. Okunsanya |
| Ug | Bishop of Soroti | A. Maraka |

## SUBCOMMITTEE 13
## THE TECHNOLOGICAL SOCIETY

| | | |
|---|---|---|
| E | Bishop Suffragan of Middleton (Manchester) | E. R. Wickham (Chairman) |
| | Bishop Suffragan of Whitby (York) | G. D'O. Snow |
| | Assistant Bishop of Guildford | L. C. Usher-Wilson |
| US | Bishop of Erie | W. Crittenden (Secretary) |
| | Bishop of Oregon | J. W. F. Carman |
| | Bishop Suffragan of California | G. R. Millard |
| IPBC | Bishop of Chota Nagpur | S. A. B. D. Hans (Vice-Chairman) |
| Aus | Bishop of Ballarat | W. A. Hardie |
| WI | Bishop of British Honduras | B. N. Y. Vaughan |

## SUBCOMMITTEE 14
## URBANIZATION AND THE METROPOLIS

| | | |
|---|---|---|
| E | Bishop of Lichfield | A. S. Reeve |
| | Bishop Suffragan of Birkenhead (Chester) | E. A. J. Mercer |
| | Bishop Suffragan of Hertford (St Albans) | A. J. Trillo (Secretary) |
| | Bishop Suffragan of Horsham (Chichester) | S. W. Phipps |
| I | Bishop of Connor | R. C. H. G. Elliott |
| US | Bishop of Honolulu | H. S. Kennedy |
| | Bishop of New York | H. W. B. Donegan |
| | Bishop Suffragan of Long Island | C. W. MacLean |
| | Bishop Suffragan of South Florida | J. L. Duncan |
| Can | Bishop of Calgary | M. L. Goodman |
| | Bishop of Edmonton | W. G. Burch |
| Aus | Bishop of Newcastle (N.S.W.) | J. A. G. Housden (Chairman) |
| | Bishop of Northwest Australia | H. A. J. Witt |
| NSKK | Bishop of Tokyo | D. M. Goto (Vice-Chairman) |

## PREAMBLE

What has the Church to say, in this time of turmoil and upheaval? What does the Church's faith, deeply rooted in history and tradition, enable it to affirm in an age when all that it stands for is being challenged, and its long-established beliefs are being widely rejected? Many today regard the Church as a static institution, backward-looking, concerned chiefly with its own survival. Yet history has shown that faith is not static, but is constantly renewed as God reveals himself in the changing pattern of man's experience. It is this renewal in faith that the Church needs today.

To say that the Church needs renewal is to say that it must show itself to be a fellowship of the Holy Spirit, the giver of all newness of life and truth. The Church always needs a renewed awareness of the gospel, the good news of God's love and grace in Jesus Christ; a deeper awareness of the deposit of the faith once delivered to the saints; a fresh awareness of the things that cannot be shaken. Without renewal, Christian theology and Christian institutions become as dry bones; with the renewal of the Spirit they become the lively expression of a transforming vision.

We recognize, however, that recent theological discussion, while it has been liberating to some, has been thought by others to be destructive of faith. While we have become increasingly aware that God has not left himself without witness in other faiths, this has been to raise fresh questions about the finality of Christ. Again, there are features in contemporary society, especially in the West, which some would see as heralding the age of the common man, others as soul-destroying. The question that has haunted us throughout our discussions has been how the renewal, which must always characterize the Church, will be experienced and expressed in a situation so variegated and complex.

What we have tried to do in the various committees, whose all too brief discussions lie behind this report, has been to allow Christian thinking, and proposals for Christian action, to take shape around the world's questions and the world's needs. We believe that it is in this way that God will renew the Church in faith; that involvement and contemplation will fulfil each other in a deeper spirituality.

Circumstances did not allow us the time we have wished to consider or amend a number of drafts, or to gain unanimous approval for every phrase. But we are hoping that this Section report taken as a whole may succeed in portraying an attitude and an approach that combine Christian assurance with a bold exploration of theology and society; that unite Christian confidence and intellectual and social risk. These are characteristics that belong to the pilgrim and the pioneer, and we believe that it is as pilgrims and pioneers that we shall show ourselves members of a Church renewed in faith.

## AFFIRMATIONS

### FAITH AND MISSION

Renewal in faith must begin with an affirmation of faith. Our faith is in Jesus Christ, through whom, by the Spirit, we have been brought into a relationship with God our Father. Because of our faith in Jesus Christ, our Lord and Saviour:

(a) We see, with the eyes of faith, the goodness and love of God, who called the world, and everything in it, good.

(b) We acknowledge that the completion of God's purpose for the world has not yet been attained: because of sin, evil has entered the world and man constantly needs God's forgiveness.

(c) We are confident that God, who rules all things in heaven and earth, has defeated evil through the sufferings of Christ and, through his Holy Spirit, works in every man to make him perfect.

(d) We believe that, in spite of their sin, all men can respond to God's goodness and share in his power over evil; and that, in so responding, they become fellow workers with God in bringing his purpose to completion.

(e) We have learned that it is God's will to bring men to perfection not by themselves but in fellowship with each other; and that for this reason Christians belong to a community of the Spirit, called the Church—a community committed to the active expression of God's love after the example of Jesus Christ.

(f) We look forward in hope to the completion in Christ of God's purpose for the whole created universe.

This faith, which is set forth uniquely in the Scriptures and is summed up in the Catholic Creeds, develops and grows under the guidance of the Holy Spirit within the life of the Church, the Body of Christ. The mission of the Church is to bear witness to Jesus Christ as Lord and Saviour of the world, who offers all men the true fulfilment of their longings and their hopes.

### IMPLICATIONS OF RENEWAL FOR THE CHURCH

Renewal entails radical change. Much in our institutions and in the structures of our common life needs to be changed or reformed, but changes are unlikely to be effective unless men and women are themselves renewed in faith and life. The basis of renewal is therefore to be found in a deeper understanding of the relationship between Christ and his Body the Church; and in the working out in corporate and individual living of all that that implies. At the heart of all such renewal in the Church is the necessity of dying and rising again with Christ. Here alone is the source of the renewal that leads to reform according to God's purpose.

Renewal entails identification with Christ. The Christian life may be described as Christ living in the members of his Body wherever they may be. It is a life realized through death and self-sacrifice—a life characterized by openness and communion with God and our neighbour. This life is lived out by the Christian in so far as he is identified with Christ in baptism—understood not merely as the rite of a moment but as the principle of a lifetime; and in the Eucharist—understood not merely as an occasional act of worship but as the focus of a constant, reciprocal relationship with God and our fellow men.

Renewal entails identification with our neighbour. Any involvement on our part in our neighbour's affairs will lay us open to the danger of being "busybodies" or "do-gooders" unless it springs from genuine identification with him. For Christians, such identification with our neighbour is the inescapable condition of our identification with Christ. We cannot know Christ, or be one with him in his Church and sacraments, unless we are also prepared to know and serve him in the least of his brethren in the world. On the other hand, Christ is the eternal word. His humanity is perfect because he is one with the transcendent God. Without this dimension of transcendence, man does not have room to be truly human. Involvement in the true service of man demands awareness of the real transcendence of God.

OFFERING CHRIST TO THE WORLD

The words of Jesus, " I am come that they might have life and have it more abundantly", when interpreted by his own life, death, and resurrection, summarize the message which the Church should seek to give to the world today. But this message will be credible only in so far as it is authenticated by the spending of the Church's own life for the sake of the world.

Christ is "the true light that lightens every man" (John 1.9). Therefore the Christian must be the first to acknowledge that all men, when they seek what is good, are in some measure turning to this light, whether they know it or not; and that all religions, as well as arts, sciences, and any other human activities, in so far as they are good and true, show us something of God and his purpose, and can be an indirect preparation for the gospel.

The heart of the Christian faith is, and always has been, the conviction that Jesus Christ is living, and that through him we can know God and understand the true nature of man; that God entered into human nature in Christ and, in suffering love vindicated by the resurrection, showed us the ultimate power and meaning of the universe; and that love, as seen in the life and death of Jesus, is the real and eternal expression of man's true nature, so that, whenever a man lives by such love, we recognize the Holy Spirit in him.

The Christian may not draw back from the world in which he lives, however much it may be a world of revolution and rapid social change. His Lord is in the world, and there he must serve him and find him. His Lord is the source of true hope for the world and for the Church, bringing history to its true goal.

We may rightly say that there is no finality in science, in metaphysics, or in ethics, but we must also say that there is no finality in our expressions of Christian thought and life. There *is* finality in Jesus Christ as Lord. Yet even when we speak of the finality of Christ, we must not appear to deny genuine progress, as though the fact of his finality implied that our understanding of Christ, or our interpretation of the Bible, was complete. Christ rose from the dead. He lives. Every generation needs fresh affirmations and expressions of faith in the living Christ at work in the Church and in the world, illuminating the Church and the world, and offering the world, through the Church, the love which will never come to an end (1 Cor. 13.8) and which is the foretaste of his own finality.

### PRESENTING THE LIFE OF FAITH TO OTHERS

The self-giving of the Christian life must express itself in terms of decision, commitment, and service in the name and power of Christ the servant. To many people nowadays confession of faith will appear relevant and worthy of attention only if it takes actual shape as the Christian response to the realities of human need.

Man's instinct for prayer corresponds to God's fatherly care for his creation, even though man does not always recognize that this is so. Deep concern and gratitude are the raw material of prayer; and every man has a capacity for silence and contemplation, although this capacity may be unknown to him and will always need cultivation.

The theological grounds for co-operation between Christians and other men are not comprised merely in the duty and desire of Christians to commend the gospel. They issue from the recognition that God is the creator and redeemer of all men.

Because of their scriptural origin, we must never neglect the cultural forms in which, according to the New Testament, the Christian faith was originally expressed. As classical Christian norms, they provide guide-lines for the translation of the faith from one culture to another. Faith and culture stand in judgement on each other. On the one hand, faith aims to strengthen the good in culture, and works against the evil in it; on the other hand, a culture can judge the faulty and inadequate manner in which the Christian faith is sometimes presented. For example, some modern art and literature express a prophetic protest against the futility in many elements of modern society, and in so doing demonstrate the failure of our Christian faith within that society.

When the implications of the gospel begin to be understood, it is seen to make difficult demands in terms of community, faith, and love —demands that many men find themselves unable to accept. It is tragic when the gospel is refused, not as the result of direct and conscious encounter with these demands, but because of the way in which it is presented.

## THE CONTEMPORARY SCENE

The times in which we live are witnessing great social and theological upheavals. Christians are necessarily involved in these upheavals, which shake the "foundations" and challenge faith. Nevertheless, we find in them grounds for hope rather than alarm.

### THE THEOLOGICAL PERSPECTIVE

#### *The Language of Faith*

One of the factors in the contemporary scene is an urgent concern about the language of faith. It might, of course, be argued that the Christian faith is conveyed by life rather than by language. But without language life remains dumb: recent discussions have led us to see afresh that language exists only in, and for, the life of a community. We should therefore not be surprised that the Church has its own characteristic language; though this does not mean that the language the Church used in the past will serve its present and future needs without modification and development.

The Christian faith should be expressed in terms that will capture not only the understanding but also the imagination of the hearer. This will call for the creative use of picture, poetry, and parable; as well as for honest attempts to meet the secular thinker on his own ground. Neither sheer exhortation nor the reiteration of traditional phrases will by themselves open the way to discernment and renewal.

Jesus Christ made extensive use of the language of imagination. His speech was concrete, direct, poetic, evocative. In his discourses he employed much imaginative material: prophecy, legend, parable, allegory, poetry, and myth. The word "myth" in English usage suggests to most people that the story to which it is applied is unhistorical. We must be very clear that the essence of a religious myth is not its lack of historicity but its disclosure of a truth having an abiding significance which cannot be wholly conveyed in abstract terms: a truth which is too real and too powerfully present to be expressed literally.

In the same way, theology makes use of symbolic language, since it speaks of that which can never be fully grasped or told. When theology uses abstract and general terms it does so in order to organize its primary subject matter, and to render it more intelligible.

## The Insights of Psychology

Another factor of the contemporary scene has been an increasing appreciation of, and readiness to learn from, the insights of psychology. These have underlined the significance for the Christian faith of themes such as freedom, love, and fulfilment, though not without some misunderstanding. They have also called attention to the caution needed in making Christian judgements about such concepts as sin, guilt, and remorse.

Christian faith is a gift from God in answer to man's basic need for fulfilment. It requires of the whole man, in his continuing pilgrimage, such a trustful response as brings with it security, love, and significance; so that increasingly he becomes what God intends him to be. The process through which faith is recognized, accepted, and expressed involves a balanced interaction of emotion, intellect, and will, in the social context, the milieu in which a man lives. That is true of any kind of faith and therefore, even more, of Christian faith, in which man is inspired and led to a commitment that goes beyond his intellectual endeavour.

On the other hand, psychology warns us that man, in his insecurity, may place his trust in what are nothing more than fantasies. It is important to recognize these for what they are, and to distinguish them from the objects of faith.

For new insights and warnings such as these, the Christian Church must be grateful to psychology and its associated disciplines, which are helping it to a better understanding of itself and of its tasks. It is to be greatly hoped that dialogue with specialists in all such fields will continue and indeed increase, and not least where there is at first sight conflict with Christian views.

*The "Debate about God"*

In the West the theological scene is characterized above all by the "Debate about God". This debate is a lively discussion regarding the assertions that can be made with confidence about God, man, and the world. Its context is one of theological bewilderment set against the background of the challenge, the successes, and the despairs of secular civilization. Among its many causes are certain trends in current biblical and theological schools of thought, which are themselves related to the swing from traditional metaphysics to existentialism. Other causes are man's confidence in his sole ability to be master of his environment, and a widespread conclusion that belief in God on the part of Christians does not make any distinctive difference to the way in which they behave.

We recall that beneficial reformulations of the Christian faith have often arisen out of conflicts, and we are confident that out of this present travail new understandings of the Christian faith will similarly be born. We also remember that the Church and Christian tradition cannot truly be themselves if they are static. The response to the historic Christ was from the first made by men living within a particular historical environment. This must always be so. The Christian responds to Christ in the light of the changing world and the experience of his own day. If, when the world changes, the Church does not reorientate itself, it fails for want of fresh insights. It cannot communicate plainly. It loses impact. For us, who live in times of great change, such thoughts as these are liberating and point to paths of renewal in Christian vitality and relevance.

We find grounds for hope and encouragement in this "Debate about God":

(a) Since God is its subject, it is a basic debate, having a seriousness and hence possibilities for good far beyond those of more familiar debates about church institutions.

(b) The Debate has helped many to recognize that faith is not merely assent to propositions but also demands commitment, and calls for action.

(c) The Debate has reminded us that our understanding of truth is always incomplete and that our ideas of God may be "dated" or inappropriate. New exploration can in the end be fortifying and enriching.

There are indeed some aspects of the Debate which furnish grounds for pastoral concern. The impression is sometimes given that the whole basis of Christianity is undermined. A disproportionate reaction against customary and valued spiritual practices is not uncommon. As a result, Christians, loyal to their upbringing but not themselves able to reconstruct their belief, are bewildered and feel unsupported. Again, the Debate often leads to over-confident assertions on very complex and debatable moral issues. Mass communication, while it has the great merit of popularizing this Debate, tends to over-emphasize unbalanced and extreme viewpoints, making the most of startling and easily misunderstood phrases. With all this in mind we believe that there is need for far more mutual understanding and support between those engaged in academic and those engaged in pastoral ministries.

In the ferment of the Debate we find inspiration for renewed faith, arising especially from the fresh concentration of our attention on God's activity in the world, on the transforming power of Christian hope, and on the richness of God's relation to man. We believe that:

(a) Within the upheaval that has shaken the theological scene, the purposeful activity of God is manifest, encouraging us to see in new situations the response for which they call.

(b) What is revealed in Jesus Christ is not simply man's true understanding of himself but also God's purpose for human history and for the whole creation. In Christ this purpose is made evident and its fulfilment guaranteed. Man's mastery of nature does not carry with it the assurance of his future. Our confidence is in God.

(c) To consider God's relation to man without reference to the divine transcendence is, as we have said earlier, to miss one whole dimension of that relationship. Properly interpreted, the doctrine of the Trinity addresses itself precisely to the false division between experience of God as transcendent and experience of God as immanent.

FAITH AND SOCIETY[1]

The Church and its members must live and bear witness in the world. Therefore they must take account of the world as it really is. This means facing up to the realities of an urbanized, technological society, and to the effects which living in what is often called a "secular society" may have upon the mental attitudes and outlook of those who belong to it.

## Urbanization and Technological Advance

A rapidly developing, urbanized, technological society is now to be found in most parts of the world, although other parts remain agrarian and will continue to be so for many years to come. The urbanized, technological society assumes many forms, and proceeds at a different

---

[1]For more detailed study of the topics referred to in this section we commend the Report of the World Council of Churches, *World Conference on Church and Society*, 1966, published 1967.

pace in different places. In such a society, a vast scientific knowledge is being applied to ever-expanding areas of life, with dramatic effect. The process of urbanization is both the consequence and the evidence of economic growth. Short of a cataclysm, it is irreversible. It is in the urban metropolis that great decisions, affecting all men, are made, and opinions formed. There can be no looking back. Without technology, people will starve.

## The Secular Society

The growth of technological change and urbanization has altered man's basic assumptions about himself and the world. He finds himself more and more in control of his environment and less and less in need of God, whom he has come to regard as, at the most, a "God of the gaps" who will supply—or remedy—his deficiences. That is to say, man has become "secular". Consequently, the society that is emerging from contemporary changes may rightly be called a "secular society": a society chiefly concerned with this present age (*saeculum*) —and with man's mastery of his own environment. Such a society rejects any authoritarianism claiming a religious or metaphysical basis.

## Material Promise

Christians are inextricably involved in the secular society. They cannot contract out of it. It is not simply that they themselves benefit from the insights and discoveries of modern knowledge; as Christians, they believe that God is involved in the world. He made it. In Christ he entered into it and was subject to it. He is at work in it still; at work in all the social and technological ferment and upheaval, as well as in the theological ferment and upheaval which that has helped to bring about. We believe that, in this process of change, God is creating new conditions and new opportunities for the people of the world, offering them a fuller and a better life; and that he intends men to share in this creative process.

## Spiritual Opportunities

If on the material plane millions have already been liberated from want, and enjoy greater affluence and increased social amenities, man's growing "secularity" seems to many to constitute a liberation of the spirit. Many Christians hail what has been called "man's coming of age" as opening up new possibilities of a free response to God. We certainly welcome the pursuit of knowledge in all fields, and the resultant growth in man's freedom and responsibility, together with the enrichment of human life and human relationships that can and does accompany it. And we believe that, when men respond freely to God and seek to co-operate with him, their faith will be renewed, their beliefs and insights deepened, and their response as "doers of the word" made more effective.

## The Sickness of the Contemporary World

If we believe that God is present "in promise" in the process of change, we also believe that he is present "in judgement". Technology produces great benefits for man, but its misuse prevents the realization of its tremendous potential for human good. It has been exploited to make the rich richer and the poor poorer. Our cities have not yet been redeveloped to eliminate slums; indeed, urbanization has often created slums and ghettos. Two-thirds of the world's population goes hungry. Many men and women are denied employment. Knowledge and power can be used to oppress, and to satisfy human greed or pride. In political and economic matters, excessive deference has been paid to conventional wisdom and outdated institutions. Man is in danger of losing his human dignity and becoming depersonalized. Often he feels himself limited and voiceless in a world where others make the decisions that affect his daily life. We cannot be blind to the signs of sickness in present-day society—the tensions between men of different races and the pressures of, and upon, minority groups; the increasing use of drugs; the spread of violence so that it seems everywhere to be becoming endemic; the development of police states in many parts of the world; the continuing wars that divide men and nations and bring widespread misery and appalling suffering. These are national and international symptoms of the sickness that underlies the political, economic, and cultural revolutions of our age. The Church, whose members are part of society, shares in this sickness. Nevertheless, the Church must expose this sickness for what it is, and must be ready to accept and suffer hostility for so doing.

To these symptoms of sickness in society we must add features as ominous for man's spiritual as for his material welfare.

(a) The contemporary world is a world so acquainted with social revolution that men are beginning to accept the idea that violence of any kind is inevitable and even good for its own sake.

(b) It is a world of rapidly and radically changing moral values, often resulting in a "permissive" society. The values of secular man are becoming relative. This can, and sometimes does, lead to ethical anarchism.

(c) It is a world of widespread fear deriving from the massive achievements of technology and the misdirection of scientific discovery—fear of nuclear, biological, and chemical warfare and the manipulation of men's minds.

(d) It is a world characterized by lack of unity and wholeness. Whether viewed on the local, national, or international level, society appears divided and fragmented.

To such a world as this the Church has to offer the gospel with understanding and relevance.

## THE CHURCH'S APPROACH TO THE WORLD

In technology and urbanization, and even in the various forms of unbelief, we believe that God is present, creating new opportunities for humanity, and calling men to work with him to ensure that his purpose is not frustrated. By contrast with the rapid changes that have created the contemporary situation, the Church—which was once accused of turning the world upside down—seems to many to be static and backward looking. It is forgotten that the Church's presence has sometimes made for rapid and radical social change, whether intentionally or not. This has been so partly because the biblical view of reality has in some cultures been causally related to the scientific method, and therefore to the growth of technology, urbanization, and secularization. In this age above all, Christians should not regard the contemporary world as an alien order, incapable of responding to the gospel. We should have every confidence that we are being called to supply in this new world a ministry that will enable the faith and actions of Christians to be fully effective.

In the situation which has been described, faith may be defined as that act of obedience in which men are enabled to go with God into the world which he is always renewing. Through such acts of obedience, our faith is constantly renewed as the Holy Spirit reveals to us, in the environment in which we live, Christ going on before us, changing the world, and calling us to follow him.

In the doubts, tensions, and unbelief that follow from rapid change, we believe—and must therefore make it clear to others that we believe—that man is not abandoned by God. Rather, through such experiences, God seeks to give man a better understanding of himself. In this way man is renewed. He is called to learn for himself what the Bible means when it says that man is made in God's "image and likeness": to grow up into the "measure of the stature of the fullness of Christ" and to share in all God's creative activity in the world.

The Church's role in the secular society must be positive, constructive, and sympathetic. It must encourage discussion and research, and never seem to inhibit them. It must foster open relationships and increased dialogue with those who have specialized knowledge, irrespective of their faith or of their lack of faith. Those who are engaged in the struggle to advance the wellbeing of humanity should have the active co-operation and support of Christians. This must be so despite the need for Christians to be, on occasion, critical of secular presuppositions, as when they point out that man's life and status are not limited to this world. For their part, Christians must always be ready to benefit from the criticisms of those with whom they work.

In the struggle for justice and freedom, the Church must be deeply involved in the search on the part of some for nationhood; in indigenous movements for the transformation of society; in dialogue with Marxists and humanists as well as with those who control power structures, political, economic, and industrial.

In such a world as ours it is natural that youth should be consciously preoccupied with the areas of social and political disorder, impatient with adult apathy and prejudice, and in revolt against the perpetuation of things as they are; so that in many nations youth protests and revolts are becoming familiar occurrences. The Church must recognize that, even when confused and strident, the protest of youth against existing conventions and institutions often comes from a sincere desire for a well-ordered society where justice, love, and service will be found. Such protest sounds an authentic note of criticism recalling Christians to obedience to the gospel.

Where they take part in the making of decisions, Christians should engage responsibly in the ordering of the societies to which they belong. There is no structure in which the Church has not a duty both to initiate and to respond to change in carrying out God's will upon the earth—and this includes the structures of the Church itself. The Christian commitment will normally be expressed in terms of a just law and order, so that society may achieve its wholeness under God. But, whenever the law perpetuates unjust conditions, revolutionary movements can be expected. We return to this problem later (p. 81).

In this brief analysis of some of the problems confusing the contemporary scene, we have tried to show that Christian participation in their solution must be sympathetic and co-operative, for they are problems through which, as we attempt to solve them, God is working out his creative purpose. None the less, in all these problems we recognize that factor of rebellion, conscious or unconscious, against God's laws, which we call sin. These human problems are caused, or increased and aggravated, by the pride, greed, and lust of men and communities. The gospel of God's redemption is addressed to sinful men inside as well as outside the Church, for the sins we see in the world are evident also in the life of the Church and her members.

PARTICULAR STUDIES INCUMBENT UPON THE CHURCH

### Looking outward

We are told that, in spite of the increasingly rapid growth of urbanization, a great part of the earth will, for a considerable time to come, retain agrarian forms of society. The main economic activity and ethos of such societies will remain primarily agrarian, even though use will be made of the benefits of technology and the social amenities associated with urban life. In this older world, rural, sacred, and traditional, God may still call us to obedience in the old forms of faith. But the Church that lives only in that older world, and responds only to its particular demands, will not have its faith renewed for obedience in a new world. Wherever it is placed, the Church needs to turn from its inward-looking attitude and promote appropriate political, economic, and social development. And even when older conditions prevail the Church must be ready to deal pastorally with a younger generation often deeply affected by having to live in two worlds—a world represented by the home and a world represented by school and places of higher education. When people work in one world and still have their roots in another, the tension becomes acute.

### A Theology of Creation

In his relation to God's creation, over which he seems to exercise control, man is in danger of failing to recognize that he is a trustee, a steward who must render an account. This may be seen, for example, in his pollution of air, soil, and ocean, and his scant regard for the balance of nature, or the needs of future generations, and his tendency, without disciplined restraint, to use the animal creation for his own ends. A theology of creation needs to be worked out which sees Christ, the agent of all creation, as inaugurating a cosmic redemption.

### Leisure and Entertainment

The Church must seek to understand how society's increasing scope for leisure and entertainment can serve God's plan for creation. Sport is occupying more and more time in people's lives, and should be a unifying force in society in face of the divisive forces of race, class, and wealth, though even sport may provoke violent and sectional partisanship. Even more important, greater interest in the arts is now possible, with advantage to the Church as well as to society. Such uses of leisure as these can open men's eyes to unexpected meanings in life.

### Culture

When the Christian faith becomes completely identified with any particular culture the result is stagnation: the faith dies with the culture. Only by God's grace and in a new culture will it be renewed. The Church must always be sensitive to the arts and other cultural forms of the community in which it is placed, and must make discerning use of them so that they may appropriately express the Christian faith to that community.

In particular there is need for bolder experiment in adapting local and familiar art-forms and prayer-forms, as well as modern forms of expression, in the development of the Church's teaching and liturgy. We should not hesitate to give expression to exuberance and joy.

*Prayer and Contemplation*

Modern ideas about God, and the Church's increased concern to find God in the world and serve him there in serving others, have led many Christians to doubt whether prayer is still possible. Yet, in so far as they emphasize the way in which God goes beyond all that we know and yet is to be recognized as present in the midst of the creative process, modern concepts of God and man may help us to pray. Prayer can then be understood as a focusing of our attention upon God thus known and recognized, and as a realization of the Christian's part in the response of the whole creation to its maker. Such considerations may also help to explain each Christian's role in the public prayer of the Church, as well as helping us to understand vital aspects of the Holy Eucharist.

Because all else is nothing in comparison with God, and man desires to be at one with him, this very involvement in God's work in the world may, by contrast, attract towards the silent enjoyment of God's presence. For some people, whether in the world or in religious communities, the way of withdrawal will be their chief and proper means of sharing in the total life and prayer of Christ in the Church. Old age and sickness may provide special opportunities for responding to this vocation.

The clergy need to be able to help each individual to find his own way of prayer and contemplation, and therefore ought to study and know the many approaches to prayer. In order to learn and teach different techniques of prayer we need:

(a) To reappraise traditional methods, which have a greater value than they are sometimes credited with.

(b) To learn to keep still and listen to God. This means fostering each man's capacity for contemplation. In this field there is much to learn from the approach of oriental religions to silence.

(c) To develop new and modern methods, such as those of Michel Quoist.

*Co-operation with those of other Faiths*

Some faiths, other than Christianity, are experiencing a significant renewal of which Christians should not be ignorant.

In dialogue with Judaism, Hinduism, Buddhism, Islam, African and other religions, Christians must be prepared to listen and to learn. In this way their own witness to the truth of Jesus Christ will be strengthened and their respect for the faith of others will win respect for their own faith. Dialogue in words must be matched with co-operation in service.

In particular, Christians will seek for closer co-operation and understanding with Jews within their common biblical inheritance. Jews, Muslims, and Christians all look back to Abraham. This, with their monotheistic beliefs, gives them a common ground for talking together.

DEVELOPMENT FOR MISSION

In response to the Holy Spirit and in obedience to the gospel, the Church must organize itself for its mission in the contemporary world. We believe that this will involve:

(*a*) Restating Christian theological and metaphysical assertions for men living in a secular society and conditioned by its outlook, and working out with them an informed and positive response to the novel moral ethical problems of the age.

(*b*) Experimenting with new and flexible instruments suited to a complex society; with the use of a far greater variety and diversity of ministry, ordained and lay; and with the development of new structures of Church and mission, including the new concept of a collegial episcopate.

(*c*) Making full use of consultants from the social sciences and related fields.

(*d*) Employing full-time professionals as members of the integral staff of the Church, in such fields as social work, community organization, education, recreational activities, and mass media.

(*e*) Offering selective training to lay people, so as to encourage them to find in their daily life the main area of their obedience to Christ; and training and retraining the clergy so as to equip them for a ministry in a Church reshaped for mission.

(*f*) Pursuing social objectives that may benefit human beings, such as housing, education, adequate remuneration for work—working not only, where appropriate, through its own social agencies, but wherever possible through secular agencies.

(*g*) Developing joint action for mission—that is, ecumenical action—as the normal pattern for the missionary structure of the Church.

(h) Co-operating confidently with those of other faiths, or of none, who are unable to make Christian credal affirmation but who can see the secular significance of what we believe to be theological truths.

(i) Redeploying its resources of men and money for the new initiatives that effective mission requires both at home and abroad, and re-examining its policy in regard to buildings.

All these developments will call for the sacrifice of resources, which the Church must accept as a necessary condition of its mission. They will also call for a greatly increased and more efficient use of all means of communication.

## INTERNATIONAL MORALITY TODAY

This is God's world; therefore the Church must seek to bring creative vision to it and recognize in existing pressures signs both of God's judgement and his loving purpose. There is acknowledgement today of the rights of man, both in his individual and national life; more awareness of the interdependence of nations; respect for differing cultures and resentment of domination. At the same time the world is threatened by new divisive forces arising, for example, from exclusive nationalism, economic frustration, misuse of mass media, heightened racial consciousness. The Church's task is not to offer blueprints of a world society but to stress the moral obligations of nations as members one of another and to encourage the growth of an international ethos. The Church must help Christians to ask the right questions, based on knowledge of the world and their experience of the faith.

### The Church as a Supranational Community

We speak with a common conviction as members of God's Church spread across the world, bound by a faith in God's love, as revealed in Christ, for all men without distinction. The Church must exhibit its true character as a supranational society whose members can experience within the context of their own nation a wider spiritual unity. This will involve self-criticism, for, while the Church must speak, it would speak more effectively in favour of international justice and order were it united and able to free itself entirely from narrow nationalism. Nevertheless, it can maintain communications over frontiers, be a reconciling influence in conflict, and help to strengthen the trust on which society depends. The Church meets man in his need on the biblical basis of the solidarity of the human race, both in sin and in hope. We find our true identity and manhood in Jesus Christ and with one another in him. It is in this faith that we approach such problems as Race, Want, and Conflict.

## RACE

Racism denies the heart of the gospel. It asserts a separation and even a rejection by one man of another. It breeds exclusiveness and superiority. It implies that the reconciliation and the unity which are God's gifts to us by his Son are undesirable. It sets limits to the limitless grace of God by which all men may be accepted in Jesus Christ. The rise of racial tension in the world (not only between races of different colour) distorts human relationships through racial power blocs, the intensifying of nationalism by racial ideologies, the projection of internal racial conflicts upon the world, and the problem of migration. All these often create antagonism, partly on economic grounds, and threaten world conflict on racial lines of division. While these factors can be appreciated intellectually, their emotional basis remains unresolved.

Racial discrimination, as represented in the ghettos, opposition to inter-racial marriage, unfair employment practices, social ostracism, and lack of equal economic opportunities, must be overcome. This requires justice within communities and the acceptance of responsibility on the part of those who exercise power within such institutions as industry, law enforcement, and education. Nevertheless, the major responsibility and final decision remains with the individual in the person to person relationship demanded by Christian discipleship. The Church must educate itself, reform its practices, and support its members energetically when they act in obedience to the principles demanded by the gospel.

## WANT

Two-thirds of the world's people go hungry every day. Millions will die of hunger and malnutrition. At the same time the world's population is growing alarmingly. The gap between rich and poor is widening. This imminent peril to mankind demands immediate action.

The organs of government are national, but our problems are global and must be faced globally. For the Christian, aid must neither be patronizing benevolence nor a safeguard for security, but the sharing with others of what has been given by God. The Church must also be constantly aware of the spiritual consequences to people who remain dependent upon outside aid, and be alert to ways in which the recipients can share their own gifts with others. Christian people should work with others to stimulate governments to give massive aid, from tax moneys, to assist under-developed countries to grow towards economic independence within the interdependence of nations. The greatest obstacle to the relief of hunger is national and personal self-interest. It must be remembered that the affluent nations recover in interest and trade balances most of the tiny allocations they make to emergent nations.

We must recognize that, to be effective, measures require a re-examination of trade structures. In the meantime we support the report of the World Council of Churches at Uppsala calling upon the governments of industrialized countries to increase their support of developing countries to one per cent of the Gross National Product by 1971. In support of this principle we call upon the Church to levy itself, diocese by diocese, one per cent of its gross annual income as a single immediate act in order to express its concern for developing nations. Bishops should begin this process by a similar levy on their stipends.

But, however fully developed or shared, the resources of the world will be inadequate unless the earth's population is educated in the need for national family planning and given access to conception control devices.

### THE ACHIEVEMENT OF PEACE

The Christian effort for peace must be part of our response to the will of God as seen in Jesus Christ. We reiterate the words of previous Lambeth Conferences that "war as a method of settling international disputes is incompatible with the teaching and example of our Lord Jesus Christ". We repeat their call to governments to work for the control and abolition of all weapons of indiscriminate destructive power, atomic, biological, and chemical, as a condition of human survival. "Nothing less than the abolition of war itself should be the goal of the nations, their leaders, and all citizens."

However, while progress has been made in limiting the nuclear arms race, especially in the partial test-ban treaty and the non-proliferation treaty, a real threat to humanity has arisen in the repeated outbreaks of non-nuclear wars using highly sophisticated conventional weapons. These cause terrible suffering to civilian populations, aggravate the refugee problems, and bring the danger of escalation. It is an international scandal that such wars are being encouraged by proxy through the competitive delivery of arms.

Because the killing of man by his brother man is agonizingly incompatible with the ethic of our Lord Jesus Christ, we recognize anew the vital contribution to the Christian Church made by many of those who in conscience cannot participate in any war or in particular conflicts.

We recognize too that the Church has not been prepared to accept the cost of Christian involvement in the issues of human conflict or to point the moral issues fairly. We have been too much identified with our national situation to give any prophetic witness to our own people. To speak and reconcile, the Church must act more explicitly as a universal body concerned for mankind as a whole and keep open communication with its members the world over.

In many lands people are living in a revolutionary or near-revolutionary situation. There is a widespread revolt against current systems of power in most parts of the world. This revolt, often violent in its nature, is frequently a response to the less spectacular but equally destructive violence of social injustice. The revolutionary ferment of our day, as it is seen in the emerging nations of Africa, in the developing nations of Latin America, and in the Black Power movement, reflects, whatever else its motives, the primary basic human longing for dignity and freedom.

Christians need to understand the causes of these social upheavals and the reasons that lead men to seek to change the existing order in their countries by violent means. In specific situations, circumstances of such extreme oppression may arise that some justice-loving Christians may conclude that the lesser of two evils is to join in armed revolt. Christians who are unable to endorse such action must find non-violent ways of changing the existing order. We commend in particular the non-violent approach so ably embodied in recent times by the late Dr Martin Luther King. We call upon the Church to reflect deeply, and in a theological manner, upon the issues raised in revolutionary situations.

The Church's task is to interpret the gospel in terms that speak to man's prevailing sense of need, and to his thirst for meaning and hope. This caring can never be shown only in words. If it is to exercise a transforming influence in society, it must accept participation in the human situation, be ready to press for change, and to enlist support from governments and institutions. This kind of involvement is costly —the cost of a life committed to Christ and dedicated in service to man.

HOWARD RUPERT'S LAND
*Chairman*

ADDENDUM

## THE THIRTY-NINE ARTICLES AND THE ANGLICAN TRADITION

In the matter of the Thirty-nine Articles we accept the main conclusion reached by the Commission set up by the Archbishops of Canterbury and York, whose report entitled *Subscription and Assent to the Thirty-nine Articles* (1968) advocates neither casting the Articles aside nor revising them, but rather prefers to acknowledge their place in the historical context of a continuous, developing Anglican tradition. We commend the further study of this report, which recognizes that the inheritance of faith which characterizes the Anglican Communion is an authority of a multiple kind and that, to the different elements which occur in the different strands of this inheritance, different Anglicans attribute different levels of authority. From this foundation arises Anglican tolerance, comprehensiveness, and ordered liberty, though admittedly it makes Anglican theology variegated rather than monolithic, and informal rather than systematically deductive.

This inheritance of faith is uniquely shown forth in the holy Scriptures and proclaimed in the Catholic Creeds set in their context of baptismal profession, patristic reasoning, and conciliar decision. These the Anglican Communion shares with other Churches throughout the world. In the sixteenth century the Church of England was led to bear a witness of its own to Christian truth, particularly in its historic formularies—the Thirty-nine Articles of Religion, the Book of Common Prayer, and the Ordinal, as well as in its Homilies. Together, these constitute a second strand in the Anglican tradition. In succeeding years the Anglican Communion has continued and broadened this responsible witness to Christian truth through its preaching and worship, the writings of its scholars and teachers, the lives of its saints and confessors, and the utterances of its councils. In this third strand, as in the Preface to the Prayer Book of 1549, can be discerned the authority given within the Anglican tradition to reason, not least as exercised in historical and philosophical inquiry, as well as an acknowledgement of the claims of pastoral care. To such a threefold inheritance of faith belongs a concept of authority which refuses to insulate itself against the testing of history and the free action of reason. It seeks to be a credible authority and therefore is concerned to secure satisfactory historical support and to have its credentials in a shape which corresponds to the requirements of reason.

Here is the full range of the Anglican inheritance and it is in this inheritance that the Articles must be set if they are to be given their true status and significance. So, wherever the Articles are printed they should never stand alone but always be set within their proper context.

Secondly, when the Articles are mentioned or implied in any affirmation of faith required as a preliminary to ordination, or on other occasions, they should always be set in their historical context, and assent and subscription should be regarded as an expression of a determination to be loyal to our multiple inheritance of faith. Through this inheritance there emerges an authority to which a man, in giving assent, professes his Christian allegiance with reasonableness and a good conscience.

**REPORT OF SECTION II**
The Renewal of the Church in Ministry

## SECTION OFFICERS

|  |  |
|---|---|
| The Archbishop of York | F. D. Coggan (Chairman) |
| The Archbishop of East Africa | L. J. Beecher (Vice-Chairman) |
| The Bishop Suffragan of Warrington (Liverpool) | L. A. Brown (Secretary) |

## (a) THE MINISTRY OF THE LAITY

### SUBCOMMITTEE 15
### LAYMEN IN MISSION

| | | |
|---|---|---|
| E | Bishop of Coventry | C. K. N. Bardsley (Chairman) |
| | Bishop Suffragan of Kensington (London) | R. C. O. Goodchild |
| | Bishop Suffragan of Malmesbury (Bristol) | C. L. P. Bishop |
| | Bishop Suffragan of Stockport (Chester) | R. G. Strutt |
| I | Bishop of Tuam, Killala, and Achonry | A. H. Butler |
| US | Bishop of New Mexico and Southwest Texas | C. J. Kinsolving III |
| | Bishop of Olympia | I. I. Curtis (Vice-Chairman) |
| | Bishop Coadjutor of Tennessee | W. E. Sanders |
| | Bishop Suffragan of Oklahoma | F. W. Putnam Jr |
| | Bishop Suffragan of West Texas | R. E. Dicus |
| | Bishop Suffragan for the Armed Forces, U.S.A. | A. M. Lewis |
| Can | Bishop of Quebec | R. F. Brown |
| Aus | Bishop Coadjutor of Sydney | F. O. Hulme-Moir |
| SA | Bishop of Zululand and Swaziland | A. H. Zulu (Co-Secretary) |
| Ug | Bishop of Kigezi | R. E. Lyth |
| XP | Bishop of Singapore and Malaya | Chiu Ban It (Secretary) |

### SUBCOMMITTEE 16
### LAYMEN IN SOCIETY

| | | |
|---|---|---|
| E | Bishop of Portsmouth | J. H. L. Phillips |
| | Bishop Suffragan of Aston (Birmingham) | D. B. Porter |
| | Bishop Suffragan of Burnley (Blackburn) | G. E. Holderness |
| | Bishop Suffragan of Shrewsbury (Lichfield) | W. A. Parker |
| | Bishop Suffragan of Tonbridge (Rochester) | H. D. Halsey |
| US | Bishop of Central New York | W. M. Higley |
| | Bishop of Eastern Oregon | L. W. Barton |
| | Bishop Coadjutor of Arkansas | C. Keller |
| | Bishop Coadjutor of Pittsburgh | R. B. Appleyard |
| | Bishop Suffragan of Los Angeles | R. C. Rusack |
| IPBC | Bishop of Assam | A. V. Jonathan |
| Aus | Bishop of Rockhampton | D. N. Shearman |
| | Bishop of Adelaide | T. T. Reed (Vice-Chairman) |
| SA | Bishop of Natal | T. G. V. Inman (Chairman) |
| WA | Bishop of Northern Nigeria | J. E. L. Mort |
| CA | Bishop of Malawi | D. S. Arden (Secretary) |

SUBCOMMITTEE 17
LAYMEN IN MINISTRY

| | | |
|---|---|---|
| E | Bishop of Southwark | A. M. Stockwood (Chairman) |
| | Bishop Suffragan of Dunwich | D. R. Maddock |
| | (St Edmundsbury and Ipswich) | |
| | Assistant Bishop of Hereford | W. A. Partridge |
| I | Bishop of Limerick, Ardfert, and | R. W. Jackson |
| | Aghadoe | |
| U S | Bishop of Georgia | A. R. Stuart |
| | Bishop of Nebraska | R. T. Rauscher |
| Can | Bishop Suffragan of James Bay | N. R. Clarke |
| | (Moosonee) | |
| IPBC | Bishop of Nagpur | J. W. Sadiq (Vice-Chairman) |
| Aus | Bishop of Willochra | T. E. Jones |
| NZ | Bishop of Christchurch | W. A. Pyatt (Secretary) |
| SA | Bishop Suffragan of Cape Town | P. W. R. Russell |
| WI | Bishop of Antigua | D. R. Knowles |
| WA | Assistant Bishop of Accra | A. K. Nelson |
| | Assistant Bishop of Sierra Leone | P. J. Jones |
| Ug | Bishop of Rwanda | A. Sebununguri |
| XP | Assistant Bishop of Madagascar | J. Seth |

## (b) FORMS OF ORDAINED MINISTRY

SUBCOMMITTEE 18
THE PRIESTHOOD

| | | |
|---|---|---|
| E | Bishop of Guildford | G. E. Reindorp |
| | Bishop Suffragan of Buckingham | G. C. C. Pepys |
| | (Oxford) | |
| | Bishop Suffragan of Croydon | J. T. Hughes |
| | (Canterbury) | |
| | Bishop Suffragan of Knaresborough | J. H. Cruse |
| | (Ripon) | |
| | Bishop Suffragan of Lynn (Norwich) | W. S. Llewellyn |
| | Bishop Suffragan of Willesden (London) | G. D. Leonard |
| S | Bishop of Aberdeen and Orkney | E. F. Easson |
| US | Bishop of North Carolina | T. A. Fraser Jr (Secretary) |
| | Bishop of Tennessee | J. V. Horst |
| Can | Assistant Bishop of Niagara | C. R. H. Wilkinson |
| Aus | Bishop of Bunbury | R. G. Hawkins |
| SA | Bishop of Pretoria | E. G. Knapp-Fisher |
| | | (Chairman) |
| EA | Assistant Bishop of Masasi | M. D. Soseleje |
| | Assistant Bishop of Zanzibar and | R. N. Russell |
| | Tanga | (Vice-Chairman) |

## SUBCOMMITTEE 19
### VOLUNTARY AND PART-TIME MINISTRIES

| | | |
|---|---|---|
| E | Bishop of Chelmsford | J. G. Tiarks |
| | Bishop of Gloucester | B. T. Guy |
| | Bishop Suffragan of Grantham (Lincoln) | R. S. Hook |
| US | Bishop of the Dominican Republic | P. A. Kellogg |
| | Bishop of Northern Michigan | G. R. Selway |
| | Bishop of the Philippines | B. C. Cabanban |
| | Bishop of Taiwan | J. C. L. Wong (Vice-Chairman) |
| Can | Bishop of Saskatchewan | W. H. H. Crump |
| IPBC | Bishop of Barrackpore | R. W. Bryan (Chairman) |
| | Bishop of Nasik | A. W. Luther |
| Aus | Bishop of Tasmania | R. E. Davies |
| CA | Assistant Bishop of Zambia | F. Mataka |
| EA | Bishop of Central Tanganyika | A. Stanway |
| XP | Bishop of Kuching | D. H. N. Allenby (Secretary) |

## SUBCOMMITTEE 20
### THE DIACONATE

| | | |
|---|---|---|
| E | Bishop of Carlisle | S. C. Bulley |
| | Bishop of Chester | G. A. Ellison |
| | Bishop of Hereford | M. A. Hodson |
| | Assistant Bishop of Peterborough | A. R. Graham-Campbell |
| I | Bishop of Cork, Cloyne, and Ross | R. G. Perdue (Vice-Chairman) |
| US | Bishop of Western Michigan | C. E. Bennison |
| | Bishop Suffragan of Massachusetts | J. M. Burgess |
| | Bishop Suffragan of Michigan | A. H. Crowley (Secretary) |
| IPBC | Bishop of Delhi | P. Parmar |
| Aus | Bishop of Bathurst | E. K. Leslie |
| NZ | Bishop in Polynesia | J. C. Vockler |
| WI | Bishop of Nassau and the Bahamas | B. Markham (Chairman) |
| WA | Assistant Bishop of Owerri | B. C. Nwankiti |
| EA | Bishop of Nakuru | N. Langford-Smith |

SUBCOMMITTEE 21
WOMEN AND THE PRIESTHOOD

| E | Bishop of Ely | E. J. K. Roberts (Vice-Chairman) |
|---|---|---|
| | Bishop Suffragan of Dover (Canterbury) | A. P. Tremlett |
| | Bishop Suffragan of Selby (York) | D. N. Sargent |
| | Assistant Bishop of St Edmundsbury and Ipswich | A. M. Hollis |
| I | Bishop of Meath | R. B. Pike |
| US | Bishop of Rochester (U.S.A.) | G. W. Barrett |
| | Bishop Coadjutor of Southern Virginia | D. S. Rose (Secretary) |
| | Assistant Bishop in the Diocese of Pennsylvania | A. Y. Y. Tsu |
| Can | Bishop of Nova Scotia | W. W. Davis (Chairman) |
| WA | Assistant Bishop of the Niger Delta | H. A. I. Afonya |
| Jer | Assistant Bishop in the Sudan | Y. K. Dotiro |

(c) THE EPISCOPATE

SUBCOMMITTEE 22
THE NATURE OF THE ANGLICAN EPISCOPATE

| E | Bishop of Rochester (U.K.) | R. D. Say (Vice-Chairman) |
|---|---|---|
| | Bishop of Truro | J. M. Key |
| | Bishop Suffragan of Colchester (Chelmsford) | R. N. Coote |
| W | Bishop of Monmouth | E. S. Thomas |
| I | Bishop of Derry and Raphoe | C. J. Tyndall |
| US | Bishop of Bethlehem | F. J. Warnecke |
| | Bishop of Fond du Lac | W. H. Brady |
| | Bishop of Louisiana | G. McA. Jones |
| | Bishop Suffragan of Virginia | S. B. Chilton |
| Aus | Bishop of Bendigo | R. E. Richards |
| SA | Bishop of Johannesburg | L. E. Stradling (Secretary) |
| | Bishop of St Helena | E. M. H. Capper |
| NSKK | Bishop of Osaka | M. T. Koike |
| WA | Bishop of Lagos | S. I. Kale (Chairman) |

SUBCOMMITTEE 24
OVERSIGHT AND DISCIPLINE

| E | Bishop of St Albans | E. M. Gresford Jones (Chairman) |
|---|---|---|
| | Bishop of Sheffield | F. J. Taylor |
| | Bishop Suffragan of Repton (Derby) | W. W. Hunt |
| US | Bishop of Eau Claire | W. W. Horstick |
| | Bishop of Kansas | E. C. Turner |
| | Bishop of Mississippi | J. M. Allin |
| | Bishop of Northwest Texas | G. H. Quarterman |
| | Bishop of Okinawa | E. L. Browning |
| | Bishop Coadjutor of Louisiana | I. B. Noland (Vice-Chairman) |
| | Bishop Suffragan of Honolulu | E. L. Hanchett |
| IPBC | Bishop of Colombo | C. H. W. de Soysa (Secretary) |
| SA | Bishop of Grahamstown | G. L. Tindall |
| EA | Bishop of Morogoro | G. Chitemo |
| | Bishop of Zanzibar and Tanga | Y. Jumaa |

This is God's world. The whole people of God exists as the Church for God and for the world, not for the sake of the Church. This is the essence of the Church's ministry. The heart of the gospel is that in Christ there is a new creation. By his death and resurrection he has broken the power of sin and death and set loose in the world unlimited powers of renewal. To be a Christian is to accept with Jesus the way of self-emptying in order to share with him the powers of this new age. Thus all ministry is sacred ministry, whether it manifests itself within the ordered life of the Church or through its service of compassion and reconciliation in the world.

Alike in confirmation and at the ordering of deacons, priests, and bishops, the gift of the Holy Spirit is invoked for the work of ministry to which the whole Body of Christ is called.

"Let this mind be in you which was also in Christ Jesus, who . . . took upon him the form of a servant . . . humbled himself, and became obedient unto death". As Christ's followers walk this lowly way, they will find authority for their ministry, and gain a sensitivity to the Holy Spirit's promptings which will issue in a life fashioned after the pattern of the Lord himself.

In order that it may be what it is called to be, the Church is equipped by Christ with leaders, beginning with the apostles whom he chose from among the first disciples. The pattern of this leadership is given by Christ himself. They are to be servants of their brethren, carrying about the dying of the Lord Jesus in order that the life of Jesus may be seen in them. By their ministry they are to equip the whole Church for ministry, so that the whole Church, in all its lay members serving the world in their daily work, may become an effective sign and instrument of God's purpose to renew his whole creation.

We must see within the context of this total ministry of Christ the varied ministries of lay men and women, of deacons and priests, and of the episcopate which is called to lead the Church in its fulfilment of Christ's universal commission, as servants of the servant Lord and servants of men for his sake.

In the whole extent of the Anglican Communion there is a diversity of cultures and patterns of human society. We should expect to find— and we should encourage—a corresponding diversity in forms of ministry. In some provinces no place can be found for a permanent diaconate; in others there is a clear need for it. In some provinces there is a strong case for women being ordained to the priesthood; in others this would not yet be consonant with the character of the culture in which the Church is at work.

This report on Renewal in Ministry must therefore reflect, in contemporary forms, the abiding truth that "there are differences of ministries, but the same Lord". To work that out in the latter part

of the twentieth century calls for adaptability and daring. To hear
(that is, to obey) "what the Spirit says to the churches" is a demanding
operation.

There is no human merit in God's gift of ministry. When God
calls and men and women respond, God enables their ministry to be
done to his glory, and in that ministry they find their fulfilment.

The various patterns of ministry, ordained and lay, are thus equal;
we cannot rightly speak of an "inferior office" if that office is where
God wants his servant to be.

This ministry in the world, to the world, and for the world, demands
that the Church corporately, and Christians individually and in groups,
face the problem of the right use of the resources which God has
placed at man's disposal. How are these resources to be received and
used responsibly and creatively? The Church must be rich in the
resources of grace and wise in the use of human and material
resources for her ministry. The Church must be poor in avoiding
dependence upon, or seeking after, riches and resources for the sake
of herself or of Christian groups and individuals.

We begin this report with a consideration of the renewal of the
ministry of the laity because we believe that it is here that the greatest
spiritual and human resources of the ministry of the whole Church
reside. From this we go on to the ordained ministry, which is concerned with the building up of the whole Church in Christian ministry.
We are concerned for the renewal of this pattern in its threefold
ministry of deacon, priest, and bishop in relation to the renewal of
the Church's ministry to the world. Our discussions have led us to
conclude that the Church has a need for supplementary ministries
differing from the lay ministry as such, yet not fitting into the cur-
rently received pattern of the ordained ministry. We gladly recognize
and pay tribute to the admirable service given by Readers in large
areas of the Anglican Communion; at the same time we see a need for
developments in ministry which go beyond any of the existing forms.

We cannot expect uniformity in a developing situation. What we
are concerned to do is to see all aspects of ministry in the Church
clearly and consciously related to the one ministry of Christ.


## LAYMEN AND LAYWOMEN

### The Ministry of the Laity

The ministry of the laity—men and women—is an integral part of
the whole ministry of the Church to the world. Man today has
enormous power over things and society. The Church's task is to
promote fullness of life and to challenge all that cramps it. It is

Christians in their daily life who bear responsibility for this task. The clergy and the laity complement each other. The laity in their daily work are generally in immediate contact with more of their fellows and, therefore, bear the greater responsibility.

## Men and Things

We are now given immense opportunities of using *things* properly, and in so doing to develop the possibilities of man's *spirit*. We must not allow men to be overcome by things nor to go on living poverty-stricken lives because the possibilities in the use of things are not developed. The material and the spiritual must be brought to a unity in the service of man under God. Many problems of human living today arise from the sheer rate of change. We have not yet discovered how to deal with the possibilities given to us. Other problems arise from the disturbed and sinful way in which men handle their opportunities and difficulties.

## Facing the Problems

Differences of race, class, and sex lead to injustice, exploitation, and destructive conflict, taking different forms in different societies and cultures. In each of them there is an opportunity for the Christian to exhibit the compassionate love of Christ. To do this he must learn to alter his own attitudes and feelings and to help others to change theirs. Groups and individuals must be concerned to study their own situations, to discover what can be done and to do it. The layman cannot look to priest or Church for ready-made answers or blue-prints for action. The decisions can only be made *by* the layman *in* the situation. He cannot escape the burden of decision nor the thought, "Any change in this society must come, in part at least, from me".

He represents the reconciling Christ, the listening Christ, the caring Christ, to those with whom and for whom he works. He himself has been accepted by God: he must accept others. In a dehumanized world, he bears witness to the infinite value in God's eyes of every human being.

## Conflict

In this continual wrestling with the opportunities and tasks of his discipleship the Christian must bear two points in mind. First, conflict is not necessarily a bad thing. The question is how conflict can be made to be creative and not destructive. Secondly, Christians will not always agree about what to do. In such a situation it is important to remember that *all* are in Christ. It is his love for all men which should arouse our concern and shape its direction. Our actions may be mistaken or inadequate; our ultimate hope in their effectiveness lies in the overall activity of God as we try to respond to it.

## God and Power

The various kinds of power in the contemporary world need to be understood and used positively. Lay men and women who hold positions of responsibility great or small, both in society and in the Church, must learn how to make their decisions in the light of their Christian faith. This is as true of the village councillor as it is of the politician or the executive. God the Holy Spirit is at work among men. He will help them to discern the truth as they honestly study the facts, as they weigh the alternatives, as they judge, decide, and act. The Christian will recognize that in this process as well as in his prayers he meets the living Christ, who came to bring fullness of life.

## Mission and Vocation

In his own country and abroad the Christian layman has a vocation to engage in mission. He cannot avoid being a good or bad advertisement for Christianity. It is easy to see the work of doctors, teachers, parents, and the like as a Christian vocation. In industry and commerce this may not be so easy. There are many who try to reshape the industrial world in accordance with the spirit of Christ: there are also many who feel powerless, caught in the cogs of an impersonal machine. Others have to support their families by work that is parasitical. Any profession, including the episcopate, can be used for selfish ends; equally, all provide opportunities of caring for others. A man may be called to stay in work involving moral tensions in order that he may influence it for good. God works through him in creating, transforming, and sustaining.

## Lay Action

A Christian layman's actions will include some of the following:
1.  Bringing Christian insights to bear on the decisions he and others constantly have to make at work, in the home, and in daily life.
2.  Helping to formulate public and political opinion on the great social and moral issues of the day, such as war and peace, race relations, world hunger, social justice.
3.  Using his knowledge and skills for the benefit of the whole com-

munity. This can range from the use of the mass media of communication to being active in a village council.

4. Engaging in direct Christian witness. He has the responsibility of sharing with others the experience of God's love. The Church should make a fresh study of the psychology of mission and new methods of proclaiming the gospel, and encourage courageous experiment by individuals and groups.

*Priorities*

For the layman responsibilities in the world are not less important than responsibilities in the life of the congregation. The Church should welcome the taking over by society of many of the functions it used to perform itself, for example in education, social work, and hospitals. Laypeople are to be encouraged to see work within these structures as part of their Christian vocation.

*The Agenda*

Care must be taken to let the laity have freedom of initiative. There is a demand on their part for a much deeper involvement in the situations in which the laity and their non-Christian fellows actually are. What the gospel has to say and what the Church has to give must be in answer to the actual ways in which people experience problems and feel with regard to them. To speak with authority requires careful *listening* and *attention* to what is going on.

*Education and Training for Work in the World*

No one wants untrained troops. Anglicans pay lip service to training, but in fact it has generally stopped by the age of fifteen. We need a Christian education explosion comparable to that in the secular world.

1. Traditional training methods—sermons, Sunday schools, day schools, baptism and confirmation preparation—need renewal through the use of modern methods. These start from the experience of the student and give him an active part in the training process. The aim is to prepare him for service in the world and in the Church. It must therefore include the understanding of the world—our neighbours, other faiths, modern technology, ourselves—as well as the understanding of our own faith, prayer, and worship.

2. The layman must be continually renewed by corporate Bible study, prayer, and sacraments. Training in prayer is needed, and for some, especially the aged and the housebound, this may be the main

contribution they are able to make to mission.

3. Christian education is a continuing process. We particularly draw attention to the need for more lay institutes. Wherever possible they should be ecumenical, since the layman in his place of work is *always* in an ecumenical situation. Often the best help the layman can receive is that given by other laymen facing the same problem. They should also be places where he can meet those of other faiths or none. In such centres the clergy will also find that they themselves learn from the laity how the gospel relates to real life.

4. We recommend that, where possible, clergy and laity should undergo training together; and also that, where circumstances permit, group training courses should provide for the widest representation in their membership: men and women, people of other denominations or of none, members of different races, and people in different sectors of society.

5. Today people increasingly move across geographical, cultural, and social frontiers as students, business men, public servants, and tourists, in the armed forces and international organizations. They need help in listening to and learning from those whose backgrounds differ from their own, and in making their Christian witness. We commend the orientation courses which exist in some countries which provide such help, and recommend that Churches co-operate in establishing such courses where they do not exist.

## The Renewal of the Church and its Structures

To see the role of the layman in the life of the Church, we must think of it as a society for sustaining men in their faith and mission. The local congregation must examine itself critically to discover whether it is able to meet the demands of the twentieth century.

1. The Eucharist is to be experienced as focusing the work of the laity in the world in thanksgiving, offering, and reconciling. The Church should pray in its liturgy for all who work, especially for those in areas of tension and places of decision. There has been a significant advance in lay participation in worship; indeed there is often nothing that a layman may not do except to preside at the sacraments. We would encourage the laity in this, as in all the many fields of voluntary work in which they fulfil their ministry in the Church.

2. As a congregation and as individuals, the local church must care for its neighbourhood, and for community and personal needs. It must act as the agent of God in sharing the reconciling gospel of Christ with all those it touches.

3. The local church should be a place where laymen can think through their problems with others of similar commitment, and the community where they find fellowship, strength, faith, and understanding.

4. We are aware that the vital role of the laity which we have tried to describe is not fully reflected in the structure of our Church. This report itself lacks many insights it would have had if laymen had shared more fully in its writing. There are still many places—at parish, diocesan, and provincial levels, in the choice of parish clergy and bishops—where the laity do not share in decision-making. We commend Resolution 24 to all concerned with all the earnestness we can command.

5. We are concerned at the lack of any form of commissioning for laymen analogous to the ordination of clergy, and Resolution 25 is put forward to encourage this need to be met. We commend the following alternatives as possible lines of experiment:

(a) Admission to Holy Communion and confirmation would be separated. When a baptized child is of appropriate age, he or she would be admitted to Holy Communion after an adequate course of instruction. Confirmation would be deferred to an age when a young man or woman shows adult responsibility and wishes to be commissioned and confirmed for his or her task of being a Christian in society.

(b) Infant baptism and confirmation would be administered together, followed by admission to Holy Communion at an early age after appropriate instruction. In due course, the bishop would commission the person for service when he or she is capable of making a responsible commitment.

Experiment along the first of these alternative lines should include careful examination of the bearing of this separation in ecumenical dialogue with (a) those holding to believers' baptism and (b) the Orthodox Churches. In both instances, the intimate relationship of baptism and confirmation with admission to Holy Communion is a matter of major importance.

## The Functions of the Clergy

This understanding of the ministry of the whole people of God (the *laos*) means that the special function of the priest is all the more emphasized. He is the representative of the whole Church, ordained by the bishop to preside at the Eucharist and to pronounce in the name of the Church the reconciling and renewing forgiveness of God. Because of his theological insight he has a special task in building up the laity for their task of relating the gospel to the world. He has to stand for God to the people of God who are going out to serve God and find God in the world. A clearer understanding of the ministry of the laity demands a corresponding clarity about the special ministry of the priest and bishop. The role we have tried to describe also makes immense demands on the theological resources of the ordained minister. For this he also must be trained.

## PRIESTHOOD

### Man

Man is a unity of body and spirit, sharing the sacramental nature of the universe of which he is part. He is made to have dominion over the created order, and to use it according to God's will and to his glory. God speaks to men through the events of history and seeks their co-operation with his purpose through their active involvement in the world's affairs. The offering of themselves and the world's resources to God is their priestly responsibility. Men's sin is to refuse this responsible obedience by using God's world for their own ends.

### Christ

In Christ God declares himself and his purposes. Christ represents God to men and men before God, and he restores their relationship with God and with one another. In his glad acceptance of human life and of suffering and death upon the cross Christ offers his perfect obedience to the Father on behalf of mankind, and so he perfectly fulfils the priestly vocation of all men.

### The Priesthood of the Church

All Christians are committed to sharing the sacrificial life and death of Christ in his ministry of revelation and reconciliation. (Rom. 6.3,4.) All Christians share in the priesthood of their Lord. This is the primary order of ministry in the Church to which all Christians are consecrated by baptism, and which in union with Christ they fulfil by offering the diversity of their lives, abilities, and work to God.

### The Ordained Ministry

In order that all the members of the Church may grow up into the fullness of this priesthood, Christ calls and empowers some to be priests of the priestly people. Although those called must be recognized by the Church as its representatives, it is by ordination that they are set apart by God for their special ministry. It is through a bishop, the representative of Christ and of the universal Church and a symbol of its unity, that a priest receives God's commission and grace and a share in the apostolic ministry. The characteristic function delegated by the bishop to a priest is that of presiding at the Eucharist in which all Christians, intimately united with the crucified and risen Lord and with one another, are offered anew to God. In the Eucharist the whole life of the Church and the world is gathered and expressed. Here, above all, we worship, we give thanks, and we intercede; here God's word is proclaimed and his reconciling love is imparted; here the Church is united, built up, and renewed for its mission to the world. In presiding at the Eucharist a priest is seen as an agent of Christ, of the Church, and of the bishop; for a priest as well as a bishop is a focus and symbol of the unity in Christ of all his people. This unity of bishop, priest, and people is obscured unless the relationship between them is seen to be a continuing reality.

## Vocation

God calls to the ordained ministry people of various gifts in a variety of ways, and their ministry must be exercised in a wide variety of circumstances. Some, for example, are called to a parochial ministry, some to a ministry of scholarship or teaching, some to community life. Others may fulfil their ministry in the context of professional, business, or industrial life. But whatever the circumstances priesthood always involves pastoral responsibility within a particular community.

Vocation to God's service in the ordained ministry is never the concern of an individual alone. It is also that of the Church which he is to serve and of the bishop who bears the responsibility of ordaining him. The variety of people whom God calls to the ministry must be matched by diversity in methods of training them, in which their different needs and circumstances must be carefully taken into account. Many of those engaged in training men for the ministry today are showing courage and vision in their readiness to experiment with new methods. Any period of training is also essentially a time when vocation is tested. Called by God to serve a world in turmoil, priests must be helped in their training both before and after ordination to that faithfulness in prayer and study which is the indispensable foundation of their ministry.

## The Work of a Priest

Ministry means *service*. A priest is called to be the servant of God and of God's people, to be conformed to the life of Christ who took upon himself the form of a servant. As *priest* he serves by faithful

L.C.R.—6

obedience in prayer and worship, in ministering the sacraments and in absolving sinners. As *pastor* he serves in gladly accepting the discipline imposed upon his time, his energy, and his compassion. He serves by being a sign to the whole Church of its priesthood, and by helping it through its members to grow into its fullness. As *prophet* he serves in proclaiming God's word, not only in preaching but in pronouncing God's judgement on sin and his mercy in forgiveness, and in equipping and renewing God's people for mission. Only as a priest remains close to Christ and all his members by daily persevering in personal prayer and by taking his proper part in the Church's worship can he grow in his ministry of service to God and man. A priest, himself a sinful man, is set apart by Christ in ordination to minister to Christians living within the tension between nature and grace—a tension which he shares—in order that he and they may be transformed into Christ's likeness. It is immaterial whether in his office he be described as priest or presbyter provided that it is recognized that his ministry is both ordained by Christ himself and acknowledged by God's people.

Today there are many doubts and much perplexity about the meaning and demands of a ministry which calls for sanctity, lifelong commitment, and constant renewal. Its sure foundation is the calling and abiding faithfulness of God, and it is in this assurance that every priest can find fulfilment and joy. As he perseveres faithfully in his vocation he will discover that "the work which he has undertaken and the skills which he acquires, far from being a superficial layer on top of his 'real personality', become wholly integrated with himself. If a man becomes a priestly man, he can never cease to be what he is" (Leslie Houlden).

## TOWARDS A WIDER ORDAINED MINISTRY

In order that the Church may be continually renewed for mission, there is need for a greater diversity in the exercise of the ordained ministry. Parochial and non-parochial, full- and part-time, stipendiary and honorary clergy are all needed.

In this variety of ministry the part-time non-stipendiary priest is in no way inferior to his full-time stipendiary brother. While in all parts of the Church there is a vital and continuing need for the full-time ministry, in some areas the part-time non-stipendiary ministry could become the norm. Such ministry does not contravene any doctrine of the universal Church, but on the contrary is consistent with Scripture and the practice of the early Church. From the experience of areas where such ministry has been encouraged there is no evidence that recruitment to the full-time ministry has been adversely affected.

*The Need*

The need for priests who will earn their living wholly or in part in some non-ecclesiastical occupation will arise

(a) Where the existing ministry is unable to provide an adequate service of word, sacrament, and pastoral care for the faithful.

(b) In groups and new communities beyond the reach of present parochial structures.

(c) In order that new work may be started in places and communities at present unevangelized. This may be achieved either by a part-time priest or by the release of a full-time priest for this work.

(d) In order that the development of team ministries may be strengthened.

(e) Where the financial resources of the Church are insufficient for the provision of a full-time ministry.

*Selection and Training*

Because of the particular demands which the part-time ministry will make on a man's character and faith, as much care should be taken in his selection as with any candidate for the full-time ministry. Candidates must be experienced Christians, mature in outlook, acceptable alike to church authority and to the community they are to serve. No considerations of urgency or expediency should be accepted as excuses for ordaining men to this ministry without adequate training. Such training must fit the candidate for the ministry of word and sacrament and be theologically, devotionally, and pastorally related both to his past experience and future vocational need. In common with all the clergy he will need pastoral care, supervision, and training after ordination. There is need for continual study of ways in which this ministry is used and the conditions under which it is effective.

*Ordination and After*

Where necessary, the Ordinal should be amended to provide for the particular circumstances of candidates for this ministry, and administrative arrangements made to govern their licensing, duties, and possible transfer from place to place and from diocese to diocese. Movement in either direction between the full-time and part-time ministries needs to be carefully regulated, with special attention to the motives for transfer and to the need for any additional training which such transfer may require.

Great care must be taken that the demands of the part-time ministry do not interfere with the requirements of a man's secular employment or with the claims of his home and family.

## THE DIACONATE

### The Present Position

The Anglican Communion, along with Churches of the Catholic tradition, declares that there are three orders of ministry in the Church, and that the Order of Deacons is, as the rubric states, "necessary in the Church of Christ". In practice, however, it treats the diaconate for the most part as a preliminary period for the priesthood. Is this a sufficient use of the Order, and if not, what should be its future?

### Possible Courses

Three courses of action are open to the Church: to continue as at present; to allow the order to lapse; or to promote a new image of the diaconate more closely related to the serving office portrayed in the early Church.

We recommend that our practice as it is at present requires reform. We do not in fact accord to the third order the importance which we attribute to it in our formularies. Our custom is a source of bewilderment to those of other Churches with whom we negotiate in the realm of larger Christian unity. If the Anglican Communion means what it says about the diaconate, it ought to give it a more significant place within its life.

We do not recommend that the diaconate should be allowed to lapse. To do so would be to reject our firmly established tradition; it would produce stresses in our relationships with those Churches which retain the threefold order of ministry; and it would deprive the Church of the witness of service which was an essential element in the ministry of Christ, and which is reflected in the overall ministry of his Church to the world. This *diakonia* is laid upon the whole people of God, and must be embodied and reflected in the ministry and witness of every Christian. Renewal in service thus demands a response from every member of the Church.

In the sacred ministry this universal Christian characteristic of service is specially represented. Just as every Christian must imitate Christ the Servant, so in the sacred ministry the *diakonia* of Christ is set before the Church as a quality which typifies the life of the Christian. To deprive the ordained ministry of the witness of the diaconate would be to impoverish its symbolism at the point where the greatest emphasis needs to be laid.

## Recovery and Renewal

We therefore recommend that the Anglican Communion should move towards a recovery of the diaconate as a significant and operative order within the sacred ministry. We would emphasize that to do this will require a period of education and a conscious effort on the part of the Church, since, in the light of our tradition, there will be a temptation to think of those received into this order as second-class clergymen.

Given such a renewed attitude towards the diaconate, we believe that there would be an enrichment of the life of the Church in a renewed diaconate, open to men and women. The advantages would lie, first, in a re-establishment of the relationship of the secular world to the will of God, through the liturgical action of the deacon; secondly, in the opportunity offered to persons in secular occupation to offer their work to God in the ministry of his Church; and, thirdly, in relating more closely the vocation of those in full or part-time church work to the worshipping life of the Church.

The diaconate must by its nature remain a Holy Order. It could, however, be exercised by those who for the most part are not employed professionally in the Church's service. We envisage, therefore, that a reformed diaconate would include both persons professionally employed by the Church, and persons who believe themselves called to an office in the ministry while remaining in secular life. It is to be hoped that there would be many of the latter and in such circumstances it might well be possible to dispense with the use of distinctive clerical titles and dress.

It would be desirable that candidates for the priesthood should pass through and be part of the diaconate. The fact that a deacon would be in some sense a minister of religion would be a matter for canonical resolution and negotiation in different parts of the world.

## Deaconesses

We have been asked to clarify the ambiguity in the statements of previous Lambeth Conferences about the status of deaconesses. Believing that we are justified by Scripture and tradition, we reaffirm the statement of the Committee on the Position of Women in the Councils and Ministrations of the Church (Lambeth Conference 1920) which reads as follows:

> In our judgement the ordination of a Deaconess confers on her Holy Orders. In ordination she receives the "character" of a Deaconess in the Church of God; and, therefore, the status of a woman ordained to the diaconate has the permanence which belongs to Holy Orders. She dedicates herself to a lifelong service.

We conclude that those who are made deaconesses by the laying on of hands with the appropriate prayer should be regarded as within the order of deacons.

We appreciate that, in view of this reaffirmation, canonical regulations will have to be made by each province or regional Church to regularize the status of deaconesses ordained in the past.

## WOMEN AND THE PRIESTHOOD

As society, and the place of women in it, change rapidly all over the world, it is right that a report on the renewal of the Church's ministry should include a reconsideration of whether women should be ordained to the priesthood.

### Theological Considerations

We find no conclusive theological reasons for withholding ordination to the priesthood from women as such. We think it worthwhile to make the following points:

The appeal to Scripture and tradition deserves to be taken with the utmost seriousness. To disregard what we have received from the apostles, and the inheritance of Catholic Christendom, would be most inappropriate for a Church for which the authority of Scripture and tradition stands high.

Nevertheless the data of *Scripture* appear divided on this issue. St Paul's insistence on female subordination, made to enforce good order in the anarchy at Corinth, is balanced by his declaration in Gal. 3.28 that in the one Christ there is no distinction of Jew against Gentile, slave against free man, male against female.

It appears that the *tradition* flowing from the early Fathers and the medieval Church that a woman is incapable of receiving Holy Orders reflects biological assumptions about the nature of woman and her relation to man which are considered unacceptable in the light of modern knowledge and biblical study and have been generally discarded today. If the ancient and medieval assumptions about the social role and inferior status of women are no longer accepted, the appeal to tradition is virtually reduced to the observation that there happens to be no precedent for ordaining women to be priests. The New Testament does not encourage Christians to think that nothing should be done for the first time.

The element of sexuality in the Godhead and its implication for the sex of the priesthood are complex and debatable matters. We acknowledge God as father and we worship the incarnate Lord as man. No theologian has ever understood this to mean that God is male. There is great significance in the ancient imagery of the bishop or priest as father to his family or as representing Christ the bridegroom to the Church, his bride. This is an image of unquestionable value, a profound pointer to the truth. But the truth to which it points has been expressed with equal power by St Paul in referring to his own relation to the Galatian church as that of a mother again in travail with her children (Gal. 4.19).

In view of the above considerations, are we to conclude that it nevertheless inheres in the very nature of the gospel that women are intrinsically incapable of receiving ordination to the priesthood?

## Personal and Social Considerations

We believe that many will welcome what we have said, and see in it a movement of the Holy Spirit inviting the Church to fresh initiatives. Many others, however, who might agree that theologically the question is open, nevertheless encounter within themselves real hesitations, or even positive repugnance to the idea of women priests. Such hesitations are often expressed as a fear that by invading a male preserve women would upset the traditional balance of role between the sexes. Leadership or headship is deeply felt to be a prerogative of men; child-bearing and home-making to be the priorities for women.

While an attitude of this kind, sincerely held, deserves respect and sympathy, it also needs careful scrutiny. The experience of other Churches shows that once congregations are used to a new situation they readily accept a full ministry of word, sacrament, and pastoral care exercised by an ordained woman. In fact, the personal capacities looked for in priesthood are evidently to be found in women as well as in men. The Churches which already accept women for ordination have not so far found the preponderance of men in leadership roles basically altered, while they have learned to welcome the different gifts brought by women who have been called and chosen. In any case many responsible women (such as heads of religious communities) are already performing without question functions of headship, spiritual counsel, and pastoral care in the Church.

## Cultural Considerations

Hesitations in personal attitude to the ordination of women are often related to cultural factors. The renewal of the Church in ministry must be achieved in a variety of cultural settings and environments, which differ from continent to continent, and may confront the Church with different cultural patterns within a single country. These will require careful study as we move to make possible the ordination of women within our communion. In countries and continents where women have already won acceptance as doctors and lawyers, and in business, politics, and education, their acceptance as ordained ministers of word and sacrament may well prove easier than in areas where tradition and custom still confine most women to the home. The Church should take appropriate steps to educate its members to think constructively about the issues.

## THE EPISCOPATE

### Its Nature

The bishop is called to lead the Church in the fulfilment of Christ's universal commission. Christ requires those who exercise leadership in the Church to be servants of all. Our way of exercising the office of bishop has often obscured this truth. What we do, and the way we do it, should remind people of Jesus the servant. This is true of all ministry in the Church; it should be especially true of a bishop.

The service of the bishop has its centre in the liturgical and sacramental life of the Church, in his celebration of the Eucharist and in ordination and confirmation. It is developed in his work of teaching and safeguarding the faith and in his general care for the up-building and equipping of the Church. It is concerned with deepening and broadening ecumenical relationships and reaches out in service, witness, and prophetic word to the life of the human community as a whole.

Christ who is the Servant is also Lord. The bishop is called to exercise an authority which is rooted in the authority of the risen Christ. This authority has to be exercised according to the pattern that he gave (John 13). St Paul, when he speaks of his authority as an apostle, speaks especially of his share in the suffering and humiliation of Christ. The bishop has to lead his people in their obedience to Christ, leading them and taking them with him. As a teacher he must try to evoke the creative thinking of his people. As an administrator he must call out and train their varied gifts so that the Church may move forward as one in its varied mission.

The commission of Christ is given to the whole Church. The bishop is therefore to exercise his ministry in fellowship with others. In his own diocese he must guide, teach, and serve in an ordered fellowship with his clergy and laity. He can fulfil his role as focus of authority in his diocese only because his ministry is exercised in partnership with his brother bishops and with the regional and universal Church.

In determining the size and structure of a diocese two factors have to be borne in mind. The first is that the Church must minister relevantly to men in their secular community. The second is that the Church must be a family in which bishop and people can know and love each other. It may be that some dioceses will of necessity be too large for one bishop alone to be an effective father in God to all his people. In such cases he will share his responsibility with a coadjutor, suffragan, or assistant bishop. Such a colleague should exercise all episcopal functions and have an equal place in the Councils of the Church.

## Training

While the servant character of the episcopate fulfils and brings into unity the significance of diaconate and priesthood in the life of a bishop, there are certain specific responsibilities which come to him by virtue of his consecration. In common with others called to positions of leadership, bishops should have opportunities of undertaking a course of training for their office. Where such training cannot be provided within a regional Church, it is to be hoped that the Anglican Consultative Council will make the necessary provision for bishops from a wider area.

## Discipline

The bishop has a special part to play in the necessary discipline to be exercised by the Church in the name of Christ. Authority to exercise this discipline is recognized as the bishop himself clearly submits to it. The bishop will try to ensure that parents understand and accept their responsibilities in the baptism of their children and that the sanctity of Christian marriage is upheld. Special problems presented by such matters as polygamy and the growth of sects will require bishops to consult with each other in their provinces and as far as possible to establish a discipline that is widely understood and accepted. True discipline is for the welfare of individuals and communities and is to be exercised in love for their recalling, restoring, and renewing.

## Oversight

A bishop will best minister oversight and discipline as he himself is disciplined by daily prayer and study of the Scriptures. His devotions will include intercession, thanksgiving, and searching self-examination with repentance. A diocese tends to reflect a bishop's own spiritual life and outlook, and he, for his part, is deeply dependent on the prayers and support of his people.

His disciplined use of time will involve and be conditioned by

(a) pastoral oversight and administration of the diocesan family;

(b) service to the whole community, including those of other faiths, within the area of his diocese and beyond;

(c) care of his own family and household;

(d) strict limitation of the number of engagements and responsibilities which he undertakes, with a readiness to delegate to others so that he may have unhurried time for individuals;

(e) his own reading, recreation, and rest.

Simplicity in life, humility in manner, and joy in serving should be the marks of a bishop's life.

DONALD EBOR:
*Chairman*

# REPORT OF SECTION III
The Renewal of the Church in Unity

## SECTION OFFICERS

| | |
|---|---|
| The Metropolitan of India | H. L. J. De Mel (Chairman) |
| The Bishop of Winchester | S. F. Allison (Vice-Chairman) |
| The Archbishop of Melbourne | F. Woods (Secretary) |

## (a) THE PATTERN OF UNITY

### SUBCOMMITTEE 25
### CHRISTIAN UNITY AND HUMAN UNITY

| | | |
|---|---|---|
| E | Bishop Suffragan of Fulham (London) | A. F. B. Rogers |
| I | Bishop of Clogher | A. A. Buchanan |
| US | Bishop of California | C. K. Myers (Chairman) |
| | Bishop of Guatemala | W. C. Frey |
| | Bishop of Western Kansas | W. Davidson |
| | Bishop Coadjutor of Virginia | R. B. Hall |
| Can | Bishop Suffragan of Toronto | H. R. Hunt |
| Aus | Bishop of New Guinea | G. D. Hand |
| WI | Bishop of Jamaica | J. C. E. Swaby (Secretary) |
| WA | Bishop of Ibadan | S. O. Odutola (Vice-Chairman) |
| | Bishop of the Niger Delta | R. N. Bara-Hart |
| EA | Assistant Bishop of Maseno | E. J. Agola |

### SUBCOMMITTEE 26
### PRINCIPLES OF UNION

| | | |
|---|---|---|
| E | Bishop of Bristol | O. S. Tomkins (Chairman) |
| | Bishop Suffragan of Grimsby (Lincoln) | G. F. Colin |
| | Bishop Suffragan of Hull (York) | H. L. Higgs |
| | Assistant Bishop of Wakefield | V. G. Shearburn (Secretary) |
| W | Bishop of Swansea and Brecon | J. J. A. Thomas |
| US | Bishop of Colombia (with Ecuador) | D. B. Reed |
| | Bishop of Newark | L. Stark |
| | Bishop of Western North Carolina | M. G. Henry |
| | Bishop Suffragan of Mexico | L. R. Romero |
| | Bishop Suffragan of New York | J. S. Wetmore |
| Can | Bishop Suffragan of Athabasca | H. G. Cook |
| SA | Bishop of St John's | J. L. Schuster |
| EA | Bishop of Mount Kenya | O. Kariuki (Vice-Chairman) |
| XP | Bishop of Seoul | P. C. Lee |

## SUBCOMMITTEE 27
### INTERCOMMUNION IN A DIVIDED CHURCH

| | | |
|---|---|---|
| E | Bishop of Bath and Wells | E. B. Henderson |
| | Bishop of Derby | G. F. Allen (Vice-Chairman) |
| | Bishop Suffragan of Penrith (Carlisle) | R. Foskett |
| | Assistant Bishop of Leicester | T. G. Stuart-Smith |
| I | Bishop of Down and Dromore | F. J. Mitchell |
| US | Bishop Coadjutor of Alabama | G. M. Murray |
| | Bishop Coadjutor of Chicago | J. W. Montgomery |
| | Bishop Suffragan of Oregon | H. R. Gross |
| Can | Bishop Suffragan of Georgian Bay (Huron) | H. F. G. Appleyard |
| IPBC | Bishop of Lahore | I. Masih |
| Aus | Bishop of St Arnaud | A. E. Winter |
| NZ | Bishop of Dunedin | A. H. Johnston (Chairman) |
| | Bishop of Wellington | H. W. Baines |
| NSKK | Assistant Bishop of Tokyo | K. A. Viall |
| CA | Assistant Bishop of Malawi | J. Mtekateka |
| EA | Bishop of Southwest Tanganyika | J. R. W. Poole-Hughes (Secretary) |

## (b) A REVIEW OF SCHEMES

## SUBCOMMITTEE 28
### CURRENT SCHEMES

| | | |
|---|---|---|
| E | Bishop of Oxford | H. J. Carpenter (Chairman) |
| | Assistant Bishop of Birmingham | G. Sinker |
| | Assistant Bishop of Portsmouth | L. H. Woolmer |
| W | Bishop of St Asaph | D. D. Bartlett |
| US | Bishop of Chicago | G. F. Burrill |
| | Bishop of Iowa | G. V. Smith |
| | Bishop of Upper South Carolina | J. A. Pinckney |
| | Bishop Suffragan of West Missouri | R. R. Spears |
| Can | Archbishop of New Westminster | G. P. Gower (Vice-Chairman) |
| | Assistant Bishop of Cariboo | T. Greenwood |
| IPBC | Bishop of Dacca | J. D. Blair |
| Aus | Assistant Bishop of New Guinea | G. Ambo |
| SA | Bishop of Bloemfontein | F. A. Amoore |
| WI | Bishop Suffragan of Stabroek (Guyana) | P. E. R. Elder |
| WA | Bishop of Owerri | G. E. I. Cockin (Secretary) |
| | Archbishop of West Africa | C. J. Patterson |

## SUBCOMMITTEE 29
## RELATIONS WITH THE ROMAN CATHOLIC CHURCH

| | | |
|---|---|---|
| E | Bishop of Ripon | J. R. H. Moorman (Chairman) |
| | Assistant Bishop of Guildford | St J. S. Pike |
| I | Archbishop of Armagh | J. McCann |
| US | Bishop of Minnesota | H. H. Kellogg |
| | Bishop of Rhode Island | J. S. Higgins |
| | Bishop of West Missouri | E. R. Welles |
| | Bishop Coadjutor of Western New York | H. B. Robinson |
| Can | Bishop of Athabasca | R. J. Pierce |
| | Bishop of Qu'Appelle | G. F. C. Jackson |
| Aus | Bishop of Wangaratta | T. B. McCall |
| WA | Bishop of Benin | A. Iwe |
| CA | Archbishop of Central Africa | F. O. Green-Wilkinson |
| EA | Assistant Bishop of Southwest Tanganyika | J. W. Mlele |
| Ug | Bishop of Mbale | E. K. Masaba (Vice-Chairman) |
| Brazil | Bishop of Central Brazil | E. K. Sherrill (Secretary) |
| XP | Bishop of Chile with Bolivia and Peru | K. W. Howell |


## SUBCOMMITTEE 23
## THE PAPACY AND THE EPISCOPATE

| | | |
|---|---|---|
| E | Bishop of Southwell | G. D. Savage (Vice-Chairman) |
| | Bishop Suffragan of Lewes (Chichester) | J. H. L. Morrell |
| | Assistant Bishop of Coventry | J. D. McKie |
| S | Primus of the Scottish Episcopal Church | F. H. Moncreiff |
| US | Bishop of Milwaukee | D. H. V. Hallock (Chairman) |
| | Bishop Suffragan of Atlanta | M. L. Wood |
| Can | Bishop of British Columbia | H. E. Sexton |
| Aus | Bishop of North Queensland | I. W. A. Shevill (Secretary) |
| SA | Bishop of Lebombo | D. de P. Cabral |
| Ug | Bishop of Burundi | Y. Nkunzumwami |
| XP | Bishop of Madagascar | J. Marcel |

SUBCOMMITTEE 30

RELATIONS WITH THE EASTERN ORTHODOX CHURCH

| | | |
|---|---|---|
| E | Bishop of Worcester | L. M. Charles-Edwards |
| | Bishop Suffragan of Sherwood (Southwell) | K. G. Thompson |
| | Bishop Suffragan of Southampton (Winchester) | K. E. N. Lamplugh |
| S | Bishop of Argyll and the Isles | R. K. Wimbush (Secretary) |
| US | Bishop of Arizona | J. J. M. Harte |
| | Bishop of Quincy | F. W. Lickfield |
| | Bishop of Western New York | L. L. Scaife (Chairman) |
| Can | Bishop of Montreal | R. K. Maguire (Vice-Chairman) |
| IPBC | Bishop of Nandyal | E. John |
| WA | Assistant Bishop of Ibadan | I. G. A. Jadesimi |
| Jer | Archbishop in Jerusalem | A. C. MacInnes |

(c) THE WIDER EPISCOPAL FELLOWSHIP

SUBCOMMITTEE 31a

INTER-ANGLICAN STRUCTURES

| | | |
|---|---|---|
| E | Bishop of Liverpool | S. Y. Blanch |
| | Assistant Bishop of London | C. K. Sansbury (Secretary) |
| | Assistant Bishop of Truro | W. Q. Lash |
| | Secretary of the United Society for the Propagation of the Gospel | E. J. Trapp |
| US | Bishop of Delaware | J. B. Mosley |
| Can | Archbishop of Algoma | W. L. Wright |
| | Bishop of Huron | G. N. Luxton |
| SA | Archbishop of Cape Town | R. S. Taylor (Chairman) |
| XP | Bishop of Jesselton (Sabah) | R. P. C. Koh (Vice-Chairman) |

SUBCOMMITTEE 31b

THE ROLE OF THE ANGLICAN COMMUNION IN THE FAMILIES OF CHRISTENDOM

| | | |
|---|---|---|
| E | Bishop of Sodor and Man | G. E. Gordon (Chairman) |
| | Bishop Suffragan of Pontefract (Wakefield) | W. G. Fallows |
| US | Bishop of Harrisburg | D. T. Stevenson |
| | Bishop of South Dakota | C. H. Gesner |
| | Bishop Suffragan of the Philippines | E. G. Longid |
| | Bishop (in Massachusetts) | D. J. Campbell |
| NZ | Bishop of Nelson | P. E. Sutton (Secretary) |
| WI | Bishop of Barbados | E. L. Evans |
| WA | Bishop of Gambia and the Rio Pongas | T. O. Olufosoye (Vice-Chairman) |
| | Assistant Bishop of Accra | I. S. M. Lemaire |
| Brazil | Bishop of Southwestern Brazil | P. L. Simões |

SUBCOMMITTEE 32

## THE POSITIVE IDEA OF A WIDER EPISCOPAL FELLOWSHIP

| | | |
|---|---|---|
| E | Bishop Suffragan of Bradwell (Chelmsford) | W. N. Welch |
| | Assistant Bishop of Winchester | N. E. Cornwall |
| US | Bishop of Arkansas | R. R. Brown |
| | Bishop of Connecticut | W. H. Gray (Chairman) |
| | Bishop of Haiti | C. A. Voegeli |
| Can | Bishop of Newfoundland | R. L. Seaborn (Secretary) |
| IPBC | Bishop of Bombay | C. J. G. Robinson |
| Aus | Bishop of Grafton | R. G. Arthur (Vice-Chairman) |
| EA | Bishop of Mombasa | P. Mwang'ombe |

## INTRODUCTION

We thank God for the Anglican Communion and for all that he has in his mercy given to us; but in the same breath we confess with shame our many shortcomings, for it is by no means the fit tool that it ought to be. We wish humbly to appropriate for ourselves the reference of the Second Vatican Council: "St John has testified: 'If we say that we have not sinned, we make him a liar, and his word is not in us' (1 John 1.10). This holds good for sins against unity. Thus, in humble prayer, we beg pardon of God and of our separated brethren."

We know too that unity will not be given to us unless renewal is given also. Hence the heading of our report, Renewal in Unity. It is not a fitting together of damaged parts into a makeshift whole that we seek for the Church but a renewal and purification of each part so that the whole may reach towards the One New Man promised in holy Scripture.

We wish first to give thanks to Almighty God for the remarkable advance in ecumenical relationships between the Churches since 1958, not least for the entry of the Roman Catholic Church into deep and charitable dialogue with us and with other "separated Christians".

But besides our changed relationship with the Roman Catholic Church there are other causes for thankfulness.

Since 1958 the member Churches of the World Council of Churches have increased from 160 to 231. This increase is accounted for largely by the coming into membership at the New Delhi Assembly of many Patriarchates of the Orthodox Church. During the same period Evangelical and Pentecostal Churches of Africa and South America have become members. We believe that the Ecumenical Movement has been in the past too much a western movement and that, if Christian unity is to be characterized by "wholeness in Christ", the insights and spirituality of the Orthodox and of the Evangelical Churches are necessary to it.

In three other areas we discern the same movement of the Spirit. Liturgical reform has leapt out of the studies of the liturgiologists and has become a matter of discussion and experiment in all our Churches, which have discovered how much there is in common between them of the basic principles and the basic pattern of Christian worship. This discovery has perhaps done more than any other thing to bring the laity of the Churches into ecumenical discussion and, more importantly, into joint prayer.

Indeed, our second ground for thankfulness has been the great increase in ecumenical prayer and particularly in the worldwide observance of the Week of Prayer for Christian Unity. Only against a background of regular and concerned prayer can we expect to hear what the Spirit is saying to the Churches.

The third main area of progress, which we can only mention here, has been in biblical studies. We welcome the formation of associations for biblical study, note with pleasure the full participation of the Roman Catholic Church, and urge our scholars to take an even greater part in such studies and our laypeople to form Bible study circles with their fellow Christians of other traditions.

We wish in general to endorse the findings of the 1958 Lambeth Conference, but we approach our subject with a changed perspective. We find ourselves impelled—but gladly impelled—to think first of the world. Its divisions clamour for healing and we see God's purpose for its unity as a cause even more urgent than the unity of the Church. Our perspective has also been changed by the new prominence of the laypeople of the Church who have a ministry and a voice with that of bishops and clergy. But apart from the excellent help available to us in our few lay advisers and consultants, we have not had the full participation that official lay representation would have given, and cannot therefore expect our report to be the balanced document which we would wish it to be. We have, however, tried to keep the world's needs constantly in view and are well aware of the dangers of a clerical approach. We believe that the Church is called into being to praise God and to serve him and thereby to serve the world. Unity is desirable not only for its own sake but in order that the Church may be a better tool than at present in the service of God's purpose for the world.

## CHRISTIAN UNITY AND HUMAN UNITY

We live in a world quite different—indeed radically different—from that of any previous age. Technological advance has made our world a very small place. Communication systems will soon unite, instantaneously and visually, all parts of the earth. This is but one of the factors that is tending to make mankind a single entity.

Of this new world, John F. Kennedy said: "Never before has man had such a capacity to control his environment, to end thirst and hunger, to conquer poverty and disease, to banish illiteracy and massive human misery. We have the power to make this the best generation of mankind, or to make it the last."

All nations and peoples desire a world free of human misery in any form, wherein there is justice and dignity for each person, and opportunity for his full development. The quest for this common ideal leads to serious tensions within and among nations by reason of conflicting interests in economic, political, and cultural spheres of action. These tensions, which can serve a creative purpose, are seen in some of the revolutionary movements of our times, the growing impatience of the developing nations, and in the search for national unity and progress. It is essential that the Church should recognize her involvement in this radically changing world, which it is her duty to serve. Her decisions and priority planning must be made in the light not only of Christian history and tradition but also of this involvement.

In this mission, the Church should be gratefully mindful that among all religions and beliefs, "God has not left himself without witness". It should therefore recognize and value the traditions and convictions of non-Christians, and without any surrender or diminution of its own position seek to co-operate with them in all possible ways, towards the furtherance of human unity in justice and righteousness. All men of good will are our allies.

The Fourth Assembly of the World Council of Churches has reminded us of some of the perils involved in such a venture, when it said:

> The Church is bold in speaking of itself as a sign of the coming unity of mankind. However well founded the claim, the world hears it sceptically ... for secular society has produced instruments of conciliation and unification which often seem more effective than the Church itself. To the outside, the churches often seem remote and irrelevant, and busy to the point of tediousness with their own concerns. The churches need a new openness to the world in its aspirations, its achievement, its restlessness and its despair.

> This is the more evident at a time when technology is drawing men into a single secular culture, a fact which underlines the essential truth of human nature as of one blood, in equal right and dignity through every diversity of race and kind. This unity of man is grounded for the Christian not only in his creation by the one God, in his own image, but in Jesus Christ who "for us men" became man, was crucified, and who constitutes the Church which is his body as a new community of new creatures.

The W.C.C. declaration further points out that "It is by this truth of man made new in Christ that we must judge and repudiate the tragic distortions of humanity in the life of mankind, some found even in the Christian community". However, we can only do this by heeding the biblical injunction first to remove the beam from our own eye. We can give the lead only by eradicating from the very fabric of our corporate life those elements of active discrimination and passive complacency, of denominational pride and ecclesiastical paternalism, which by their very existence destroy the unity which we proclaim. As Lambeth 1958 said, "A divided Church cannot heal the wounds of a divided world".

We are compelled to look to Christ himself for a style of life and a pattern of action, which will enable the Christian community to continue his work. But as we do so, we are immediately confronted by the cross. The same Christ "through whom God chose to reconcile the whole universe to himself" first "made himself nothing", "emptied himself", and "assumed the nature of a slave". The Christian community can do no less, and must be willing to run the same risks as its Master, offering itself humbly and entirely for the life of the world which it serves. The Church, then, must empty itself of all false pride, worldly power, and privilege, and become a servant community. Only in this way can it be an effective sign of the presence in the world of the servant Christ.

## PRINCIPLES OF THE ANGLICAN QUEST FOR UNION

The union of God with man and of men with one another is rooted in the mystery of the unity of the Godhead. In the meditation which is the seventeenth chapter of St John, Jesus prays that his disciples and all future believers may share in the unity of the Father with the Son. This union is linked with a sharing in Jesus' own consecration to the way of holiness and with the reception of the truth which Jesus reveals. It is linked with the movement of the disciples into the world in mission, "that they all may be one . . . that the world may believe that thou hast sent me". Unity is inseparable from the renewal of the Church in holiness and truth and is always related to its mission.

In the Epistle to the Ephesians, unity is seen as a growth from the unity which the Spirit gives into a fullness of life which is to be measured by nothing less than the fullness of the manhood of Christ, who is our peace and has already abolished the enmity between us. The "new humanity" in Christ is seen in the Epistle to the Colossians as culminating in the reconciliation to God through Christ of the whole created universe.

So the Church is called to be the foretaste of a redeemed creation, a sign of the coming unity of mankind, a pointer to the time when God shall be all in all. We may not speak of the limited task of manifesting a greater unity between separated Christians here and now unless we always do so in this context of the unfathomable unity of the Godhead, communicated by the Spirit as the Church is renewed in all its members in holiness and truth for mission and service to all mankind and as it awaits the final summing up of all things in Christ.

The Church of God, as witnessed to by Scripture, is both a gift of God to man and a sphere of obedience to God by men. The unity which is God's gift is indestructible because it is rooted in Christ's once-for-all reconciliation. This is apparent in history as union among men in Christ wherever faith responds by baptism into the remission of sins and by the receiving of Christ in the Eucharist. The call of God to men in history is thus always a call to that obedience which fulfils God's gift of unity in a deepening and widening union among all who are in Christ.

At many Lambeth Conferences since 1888, the Anglican Communion has sought to express the nature of this unity in Christ as both gift and calling. This expression, which has passed through a variety of formulations,[1] has come to be known as the Lambeth Quadrilateral and has always included four elements:

1. Common submission to Scripture as the Word of God, the uniquely authoritative record of God's revelation of himself to man

2. Common profession of the faith derived from that revelation, especially as witnessed to in the primitive Creeds

3. Common acceptance of the divinely instituted sacraments of baptism and the Holy Communion

4. Common acknowledgement of a ministry through which the grace of God is given to his people.

The Quadrilateral has served in part as an indication of those gifts of God to the Anglican Communion which it has received as a part of the one, holy, catholic, and apostolic Church and also in part as an indication of what God is calling the whole Church in history more fully to become.

On the basis of what God has given, including a ministry within the historic episcopate, the Anglican Communion has persistently encouraged conversation or dialogue with other Christian communions as also within the Body of Christ, "so that the ideal of the one flock under one Shepherd may be realized" (Lambeth Encyclical, 1888). The purpose of such conversation with a view to union is always in order that our life together in Christ may be wider and

---

[1] Its formulation in 1888 was as follows: "That, in the opinion of this Conference, the following Articles supply a basis on which approach may be by God's blessing made towards Home Reunion: —

(A) The Holy Scriptures of the Old and New Testaments, as 'containing all things necessary to salvation', and as being the rule and ultimate standard of faith.

(B) The Apostles' Creed, as the Baptismal Symbol; and the Nicene Creed, as the sufficient statement of the Christian faith.

(C) The two Sacraments ordained by Christ Himself—Baptism and the Supper of the Lord—ministered with unfailing use of Christ's words of Institution, and of the elements ordained by Him.

(D) The Historic Episcopate, locally adapted in the methods of its administration to the varying needs of the nations and peoples called of God into the unity of His Church."

deeper than is possible in our separation. We do not deny the reality of what God has already given us by acknowledging that true union would give to all of us that which, by our division, we lack.

As we look again at the four points of the Quadrilateral at this tenth Lambeth Conference, we see them as affirming both that which God has given and that to which he calls us.

(1) *The Scriptures.* We gratefully recognize that in the Scriptures we are given the content of God's self-disclosure, a witness to his saving Word in Christ, and a means by which the Holy Spirit speaks both to the Church as a whole and to individuals. We also recognize that the understanding of Scripture, in all its internal variety and coherence, invites all Christians to a common appropriation of its riches which none of the Churches alone has achieved.

(2) *The Creeds.* We gratefully recognize that the Church in the first centuries gave, to some basic questions implicit in Scripture, authoritative answers which are common ground. We also recognize that our generation is called to live in an epoch when "the faith once delivered to the saints" must be reinterpreted in a form which no part of the Church could accomplish in isolation.

(3) *The Sacraments.* We gratefully recognize that our one baptism into Christ constitutes a degree of union more substantially and universally acknowledged than previously and that the centrality of the Eucharist in the life of the Church is now seen in many aspects of liturgical and pastoral renewal in all Churches. We also recognize that we are all called to a deeper appreciation of the significance and implication of baptism, and also to heal the breach which has developed between our unity in baptism and our separations in the Eucharist.

(4) *The Ministry and Episcopacy.* We gratefully recognize that, in a variety of forms, God's gifts of ministry have been used "for the equipment of the saints for the work of ministry, for the building up of the body of Christ" (Eph. 4.11-12). We also recognize that we still seek "a ministry acknowledged by every part of the Church as possessing not only the inward call of the Spirit, but also the commission of Christ and the authority of the whole body" (Lambeth Appeal, 1920). We have known the grace which God gives through a threefold ministry in which bishops are called to exercise pastoral care and to safeguard historic continuity and authority within the Church. We offer this experience, in fellowship with those who have experienced the grace of the continuity of apostolic doctrine through the service of other forms of ministry, and with those who have experienced God's grace through papal authority in the episcopal college, in the faith that God will restore the fullness of ministry in ways which we cannot yet discern.

Because the Lambeth Quadrilateral has been concerned with the principles of union, it is also concerned with the renewal of the Church in holiness and truth and with its dedication to mission and service. It is not a static formulation of positions in which Anglicans are entrenched. Rather we see it in the context of the vision of unity expressed at the World Council of Churches Assembly at New Delhi:

> We believe that the unity which is both God's will and his gift to his Church is being made visible as all in each place who are baptized into Jesus Christ and confess him as Lord and Saviour are brought by the Holy Spirit into one fully committed fellowship, holding the one Apostolic Faith, preaching the one gospel, breaking the one bread, joining in common prayer, and having a corporate life reaching out in witness and service to all: and who at the same time are united with the whole Christian fellowship in all places and all ages in such wise that ministry and members are accepted by all and that all can act and speak together as occasion requires for the tasks to which God calls his people.

We accept this call to advance, in growing union with our fellow Christians, towards God's high destiny for mankind renewed in Christ.

## INTERCOMMUNION IN A DIVIDED CHURCH

The growing solidarity of Christians of different traditions in common witness to Christ and in service to the world gives new urgency to the question of their relationship to one another at the deepest levels of worship and sacramental life. Many, particularly of the younger generation, are constrained to find strength for this solidarity in common participation in the Eucharist. We look forward to the day when our God-given unity in baptism into Christ is expressed and fulfilled in our unity in the Eucharist. We believe that this Eucharist should be the worship of the whole Church visibly united under the presidency of the bishop or his delegate as the effective symbol of the Church's unity and continuity. We desire for all baptized Christians a relationship at the Lord's table which shall minister to such unity.

### DEFINITIONS

The definitions of the terms full communion, intercommunion, open communion, and free communion as given in Chapter 3 of *Intercommunion Today* (C.I.O., 1968) are used in this report and commended for general acceptance. While commending the full analysis in the Report, we give the following brief definitions of some of the terms used.

*Full communion* involves mutual recognition of ministers and members (e.g. the relationship between Churches of the Anglican Communion).

*Open communion* is the practice whereby one particular Church welcomes all baptized communicant members of other Churches to receive communion on occasion within its fellowship.

*Free communion* is the practice of inviting to the Lord's table "all who love the Lord Jesus" irrespective of whether they have a church affiliation or are in good standing with their own communion, or even whether they are baptized.

*Reciprocal intercommunion* is the occasional and reciprocal sharing in the Eucharist by members of Churches which are seeking, but have not yet achieved, full communion or organic union. This reciprocal intercommunion arises from a relationship between Churches and necessarily involves the mutual consent of the Churches concerned.

*Admission to communion* is the practice of controlled admission to communion where a particular Church defines not only its own domestic discipline but also the condition under which the communicants of other Churches may be welcomed to receive Holy Communion.

## CONFIRMATION RUBRIC

The regulation of the Confirmation Rubric concerning admission to communion raises different issues with regard to those who are members of the Anglican Communion and with regard to those who are members of some other Church. We note that, within the Anglican Communion, the relation of baptism, confirmation, and admission to Holy Communion, and the age for confirmation, are subject to review. Whatever the past history of the Confirmation Rubric, it might appear to forbid admission of members of other Churches to communion in the Anglican Church and in some provinces has been so interpreted. In practice, however, individual members of other Churches have for long been admitted to Holy Communion, and we propose that regulations for admission of such individuals should be maintained and widened, and provision also be made for occasional reciprocal intercommunion. It would be for each province to work out, according to its own constitutional method, how the rubric in the Prayer Book and the corresponding canon should be adjusted to meet the actual situation.

## ADMISSION TO COMMUNION

While keeping the goal of full communion in view, in order to minister to the unity of the Church, we believe that provision must be made for the admission of individuals to communion in a Church in which they have not formally been given communicant status. This provision is necessary to meet the pastoral needs of members of our own and other Churches in an ecumenical age and in a mobile and pluralistic world society, for instance in the following circumstances:

(a) communicants living in and visiting areas not effectively served by their own Churches

(b) communicants amongst groups of people travelling or engaged in various common enterprises, wishing to worship together in Holy Communion, but belonging to different Churches

(c) family situations and relationships where members of different Churches would naturally be drawn to common worship

(d) schools, colleges, hospitals, and other close-knit communities

(e) inter-Church activities at all levels.

In order to meet such pastoral needs of God's people, we recommend that under the direction of the bishop

1. Christians duly baptized in the name of the Holy Trinity and qualified to receive Holy Communion in their own Churches may be welcomed at the Lord's table in the Anglican Communion.

2. While it is the general practice of the Church that Anglican communicants should receive the Holy Communion only at the hands of ministers of their own Church or of Churches in communion therewith, such communicants are free to attend the Eucharist in other Churches holding the Apostolic Faith as contained in the Scriptures and expressed in the Apostles' and Nicene Creeds and may be free, as conscience dictates, to receive the sacrament when they know they are welcome to do so.

The exercise of such liberty would be to meet special circumstances and would in no way derogate from the discipline and participation of church members in the life of the Church to which they belong. It should, therefore, not weaken the loyalty of the Christian to his Church nor blunt his determination to find unity according to the will of Christ.

RECIPROCAL INTERCOMMUNION

Within the movement towards organic union in which Churches of the Anglican Communion are involved in many parts of the world, we regard reciprocal intercommunion as allowable and in many cases advisable when an advanced stage has been reached in the negotiations, and where there is agreement on apostolic faith and order. As the Archbishop of Canterbury expressed it to this Conference:

Unity is once for all given in the incorporation of Christians into Christ, but the Church grows into the full realization of unity through centuries of time. We bear in mind firmly both the Church as already given with those Catholic norms to which we are pledged to be faithful, and the looking ahead to the Church in its plenitude towards which we are moving. There is identity between the Church once given and the Church in its coming plenitude.

Such reciprocal intercommunion would precede the final stage of organic union or the unification of the ministries. Each province concerned would determine when the negotiations for union in which it is engaged have reached the stage which allows this intercommunion. We note the care with which certain provinces are determining when such intercommunion should be allowed; and we agree that the Churches concerned should have the firm intention to unite and that intercommunion should be regarded as only a temporary relationship on the way to organic union.

We recommend that where there is agreement between an Anglican Church and some other Church or Churches to seek unity in a way which includes agreement on apostolic faith and order, and where that agreement has found expression whether in a covenant to unite or in some other appropriate form, a Church of the Anglican Communion should be free to allow reciprocal acts of intercommunion under the general direction of the bishop. Such acts of intercommunion might for instance take place during Holy Week or a Week of Prayer for Christian Unity, or at special services in parishes, or at conferences where there is a real intention to forward the unity of the Church. On such occasions the Eucharist might be celebrated by a minister of one of the participating Churches, or celebrated jointly by the ministers of the different communions acting together under the presidency of one of them.

CONSENSUS ON THE EUCHARIST

In all discussion of intercommunion we are convinced of the need for continuing theological dialogue, and particularly for sharing in the present renewal of eucharistic thinking and practice now taking place amongst the Churches.

An important feature of this dialogue is the inclusion of members of the Roman Catholic Church within the membership of the Faith and Order Commission and their increasing involvement in its work. In the light of Vatican II, the question of intercommunion belongs to an ecumenical dialogue involving the Roman Catholic Church.

Whenever intercommunion is proposed between Churches we believe that there should first be found a basic agreement on the meaning of the Eucharist. Any consensus between Churches should include mention of those essential elements to be found in any service of the Eucharist. We commend strongly to our Churches the study of a résumé of the Emerging Consensus on the Eucharist published by the Faith and Order Commission of the World Council of Churches.

CORPORATE DECISIONS OF THE CHURCHES OF OUR COMMUNION

We realize that some members of our communion will not be able to reconcile their consciences to such liberty as is proposed in this report.

However, we believe that the various Churches of our communion may desire to make corporate decisions which will claim the loyalty of all their members, and at the same time show such proper regard for those members who in conscience cannot accept them that their fellowship within the Church is unimpaired.

## THE CHURCH OF SOUTH INDIA

We urge all Churches of the Anglican Communion initially to re-examine their relation to the Church of South India, particularly with regard to any restriction on bishops and episcopally ordained ministers of the Church of South India who visit a diocese exercising their ministry in those Churches with which the Church of South India is in communion.

Further, since the Church of South India is showing itself to be an episcopally ordered Church, and all its members are in communion with the bishop, we believe that the way is now open for Churches of the Anglican Communion to establish full communion with the Church of South India.

## CURRENT SCHEMES

Since 1958 the movement towards the formation of schemes of union has gathered momentum. Three schemes have now reached the point of final decision by the Churches concerned: the plan for the Church of North India/Pakistan, the scheme for the Church of Lanka (Ceylon), and the scheme for full communion between Anglicans and Methodists in Great Britain.

Elsewhere Anglicans are involved in discussions and plans for union which have not yet reached their final formulation but on which there are published documents available: in England and Scotland (with the Presbyterian Church of England and the Church of Scotland), Canada, Ghana, the U.S.A., New Zealand, the West Indies, and Zambia. Conversations have also begun in Wales and Ireland and many other inter-Church talks are going on, in some of which Anglicans are not involved.

### Nigeria

We were reminded of the last-minute postponement of the inauguration of the proposed Church of Nigeria and have noted that in the present political situation no resumption of the discussions has been possible. We wish to express our sympathy, and we hope that an early return of peace to the area will enable negotiations to be resumed in such form as may then be practicable.

### North India/Pakistan and Lanka (Ceylon)

The plan for the Churches of North India and of Pakistan is now before the negotiating Churches in its final form, some of which have already given it full approval. We note that as a result of further progress in the negotiations as reflected in the fourth revised edition of the Plan (1965) difficulties which had been a matter of concern to the 1958 Lambeth Conference have been overcome. We understand that the plan is likely to receive the full approval of the General Council of C.I.P.B.C. at its next meeting at the beginning of 1970. We hope that the union will come into operation at an early date.

The Conference of 1958 expressed the definite hope that the scheme for the Church of Lanka would go forward. We are glad to learn that it is expected that the scheme will have passed through all the stages of approval in the course of the next two or three years. We recommend that Churches of the Anglican Communion should enter into full communion with the Churches of North India and Pakistan and with the Church of Lanka, and should foster the relations of fellowship which this involves.

*Anglicans and Methodists in Great Britain*

We have given careful consideration to the proposals set out in the two parts of the final report of the Anglican–Methodist Unity Commission, 1968. The Conference of 1958 in Resolution 30 (p. 1.38) gave encouragement to the two Churches to continue negotiations "on the understanding that organic union is definitely accepted as the final goal, and that any plans for the interim stage of intercommunion are definitely linked with provisions for the steady growing together of the Churches concerned". We note that it is an integral part of the present proposals that the two Churches should commit themselves from the beginning of Stage One to the achievement of organic union at Stage Two of their new relationship.

We draw the attention of the Conference to the vital significance of the proposed coming together of these two Churches in Great Britain. Their separation has had far-reaching consequences for the development of the Church in other lands. The healing of this breach in Great Britain is likely to be influential for the relations of Anglicans and Methodists in many other parts of the world.

We recognize that the proposal for a stage of full communion to precede the final stage of organic union arises out of the peculiar historical circumstances of the Church in Great Britain, more especially of the Church of England. This two-stage procedure is not necessarily recommended for other areas. The report urges that in the stage of full communion the two Churches should take every step to grow together by common consultations, common action, and common devotion at all levels. According to the proposals, the Methodist Church will accept the historic episcopate and the rule of episcopal ordination for the future, and there will be an Ordinal for common use by the Churches from the beginning of Stage One. We judge that the proposed Service of Reconciliation is theologically adequate to achieve its declared intentions of reconciling the two Churches and integrating their ministries. In our view, if the proposals are accepted by both Churches, sufficient agreement in faith and order will exist between them to justify a relation of full communion.

We think that the undoubted excellence of the new proposed Ordinal greatly strengthens the acceptability of the proposals and that this Ordinal may well attract the attention of other Churches engaged in negotiations or liturgical revision.

UNIFICATION OF MINISTRIES

In the three final schemes mentioned above provision is made for the unification of the ministries at the inauguration of the union. In each case the acts of unifying or reconciling the ministries are set in the context of, and follow upon, acts which inaugurate the union of the Churches concerned, or, in the case of the Anglican–Methodist scheme, the act by which the two Churches accept one another into full communion and declare their resolve ultimately to unite in one Church. This order of liturgical acts, we believe, puts the unification of the ministry in its proper setting.

The Conference of 1948 gave counsel that "The unification of the ministry in a form satisfactory to all the bodies concerned, either at the inauguration of the union or as soon as possible thereafter, is likely to be a prerequisite to success in all future proposals for the reunion of the Churches" (Resolution 56, 1.40). We believe that the three schemes mentioned above have provided for the unification or reconciliation of the ministries in a comprehensive and inclusive way which meets the desire for the integration of the ministry with the historic episcopate without involving the Churches concerned in any repudiation of the ministries which they have hitherto exercised. There is a further purpose in these liturgical acts. An integral part of their intention and of the scope of their central petition is the submission into the hands of God of all the ministries concerned and the invocation of a fresh gift of God to each and all, according to their need, for the work to which they are now called in unity and reconciliation.

Other negotiations now in progress also appear to contemplate a unification of the ministries at the inauguration of union, following the advice of the 1948 Conference. Though we think this advice should continue to receive serious attention, we do not wish it to be regarded as excluding other procedures, differing from it whether in character or in detail. We are aware that movements of theological thought about the ministry and its relation to the Church are taking place in the Christian world, including the Roman Catholic Church, and may, if they result in generally acceptable conclusions, lead to other approaches to the question of unity as it affects the ministry of the uniting Churches.

We turn to make brief comments on conversations now in progress.

*Ghana*

We were glad to learn of good progress in the negotiations and would like to encourage the diocese of Accra to go forward with the development of this promising scheme. In the important matter of securing due influence to the bishops in safeguarding the faith of the Church, we recognize that this can be provided for in different ways and that bishops are to share this responsibility with other organs of the Church. We agree that the steps proposed to give the bishops their due part in this in Ghana are sufficient. The service for the unification of the ministry was not before us in its final form, but after seeing the present draft, and in the interest of the widest possible measure of communion with other Churches desired by the Ghana Church as by us all, we would like to call attention again to what was said by the last Lambeth Conference on the whole question of the prayer to be said before the laying on of hands and of any formula to be used at it (*Lambeth Conference 1958*, 2.36-8).

*Canada*

The Anglican Church of Canada has been in conversation with the United Church of Canada, and in a booklet entitled *The Principles of Union* has published the principles agreed upon by the governing bodies of both Churches. These principles follow the lines with which we are now familiar in other parts of the world and seem to give promise of very satisfactory fruit. It is noteworthy that before expressing its acceptance the Anglican Church sent the documents to the dioceses for study. It is gratifying to hear that a Joint General Commission and certain Joint Special Commissions have been set up to prepare a scheme of union.

*U.S.A.*

Conversations are also in progress in the U.S.A. A summary of the basic principles so far agreed upon has been published in *A Consultation on Church Union*. The situation in this country is complicated in as much as no fewer than nine Churches are involved. We warmly endorse the verdict of the General Convention of the Episcopal Church in 1967, which commended the Principles of Church Union as "a significant advance towards Christian unity in certain matters of doctrine, worship, sacraments and ministry", and we are

pleased to note that the Joint Commission on Ecumenical Relations
has been authorized to participate in the development of a proposed
plan of union for study at all levels of church life.

### Anglicans and Presbyterians in England and Scotland

We had before us the report *Relations between the Church of England
and the Presbyterian Church of England* (1968). This document con-
tains clear and valuable discussion of issues relating to the doctrine of
the Church, its mission, unity, and ministry. It would provide useful
guidance for discussions in other parts of the world. Conversations are
also going on between Presbyterians and Congregationalists in England
parallel to those between Anglicans and Methodists, and we endorse
the hope expressed in the last four paragraphs of the report for a
comprehensive union of all these Churches. A report of 1966 spoke of
"a united Church in England and a united Church in Scotland in full
communion with each other" as the ultimate goal. We trust that this
goal will be reached as the final outcome of the conversations in
England and the continuing discussions between the Church of Scotland and the Episcopal Church in Scotland and other Churches in that
country.

### New Zealand

There is a Joint Commission of the Church of the Province of New
Zealand and of four other Churches. It issues an annual report on
matters concerning union which the Church of the Province has
referred to the dioceses for their comment and approval. In this way
the progress of discussions at the higher level is made known to the
clergy and people of the dioceses and they themselves become involved
in the discussion. Steady progress is now being made towards the
drawing up of a Basis of Union for submission to the Churches in the
near future.

### West Indies

The report of the Anglican–Methodist consultation in the West Indies
has been circulated to the dioceses of the province and is awaiting
their comments. This follows closely the two-stage plan proposed between the two Churches in Great Britain and we suggest that at a later
revision account might be taken of changes made in the English
scheme in its final form. We encourage the two Churches to go
forward. We note that there are dioceses of the Episcopal Church
in the United States in the area which are not at present involved in
the discussions, and we recommend that reports of these consultations
be forwarded to such dioceses. Any final plans should involve all
Anglican dioceses in the area. We think that this principle should be
applied everywhere.

## Zambia

The discussions in Zambia between the Anglican diocese of Zambia and the United Church of Zambia are still at an early stage. The draft basis of union is one that we can commend and we hope that it will provide the ground for successful negotiations.

## Ireland

We learn with interest that the Church of Ireland, the Presbyterian Church, and the Methodist Church in that country have officially accepted a common Declaration of Intent to work together and to seek unity.

## Wales

We are glad to know that the Church in Wales has taken part in conversations sponsored by the Council of Churches for Wales about the implications and terms of a Covenant between the Churches.

## The Moravian Church

The Conference of 1948 expressed a hope for continued conversations with this Church. We note with regret that these conversations have lapsed and trust they will be reopened.

In examining the several reports of discussions and conversations we note with warm approval the cross-references to other schemes, and we urge that in each area those taking part in conversations should continue to be fully aware of what is happening elsewhere in the Anglican Communion and among Christians everywhere.

# RELATIONS WITH THE ROMAN CATHOLIC CHURCH

In the "Common Declaration", signed in Rome on 24 March 1966, the Pope and the Archbishop of Canterbury gave thanks to Almighty God for the new atmosphere of Christian fellowship now existing between the two Churches, and declared their intention of inaugurating "a serious dialogue which, founded on the Gospels and on the ancient common traditions, may lead to that unity in truth, for which Christ prayed". This dialogue, they declared, was to include "not only theological matters such as Scripture, Tradition and Liturgy, but also matters of practical difficulty felt on either side".

It was as a result of this Declaration that a Joint Preparatory Commission was set up; and the Section received with gratitude the report issued as a result of the three meetings of that Commission.

Essential to such meetings is the spirit in which they are undertaken. For our part we recognize in penitence that many of our past attitudes and actions have contributed to our unhappy divisions and that there are still many things in us for which we must ask the forgiveness of God and of our fellow Christians. Yet we are thankful for the many signs of renewal of the spirit of unity in ourselves and in others.

Together with the Roman Catholic Church we confess our faith in God, Father, Son, and Holy Spirit, as witnessed by the holy Scriptures, the Apostles' and Nicene Creeds, and by the teaching of the Fathers of the early Church. We have one baptism and recognize many common features in our heritage. At the same time substantial divergences exist, many of which have arisen since the sixteenth century, in such matters as the unity and indefectibility of the Church and its teaching authority, the Petrine primacy, infallibility, and Mariological definitions, as well as in some moral problems. These matters will require serious study so that they may be carefully identified and, under the guidance of the Spirit, resolved. This task must be undertaken in the light of the challenge to the whole Church of God presented by the modern world, and in the context of the mission of the Church throughout the world and to all sorts and conditions of men.

SIGNS OF PROGRESS

Relations between Anglicans and Roman Catholics are progressing in various ways and to varying degrees in many places. Examples include common services of prayer and thanksgiving, the joint use of churches, the exchange of preachers, co-operation in theological education, and meetings of official commissions and informal groups. With due regard to individual consciences, we endorse and encourage these developments where local circumstances permit the avoidance of misunderstanding.

We rejoice that the new attitude towards Scripture, expressed in the Constitution on Divine Revelation, has led to co-operation in biblical studies and in the work of the United Bible Societies.

Liturgical renewal and reform represent a field where co-operation is urgent. Unilateral action in regard to the liturgical year and the vernacular forms used by our people is to be avoided.

The Christian witness being given by our clergy and laity in many urgent human issues, in many cases in close association with Roman Catholics, claims our support and our prayers. Where such witness may be strengthened by joint or parallel statements by church leaders, these should be issued.

We welcome the increasing signs of mutual recognition, not least in practical acts on both sides, of the reality of Anglican and Roman Catholic ministry in the whole Body of Christ on earth.

A PERMANENT JOINT COMMISSION

We recommend the setting up of a Permanent Joint Commission, our delegation to be chosen by the Lambeth Consultative Body or its successor and to be representative of the Anglican Communion as a whole. This commission or its subcommissions should consider the question of intercommunion in the context of a true sharing in faith and the mutual recognition of ministry, and should also consider in the light of the new biblical scholarship the orders of both Churches and the theology of ministry which forms part of the theology of the Church and can only be considered as such. The hope for the future lies in a fresh and broader approach to the understanding of apostolic succession and of the priestly office. On this line we look for a new joint appraisal of church orders.

Conversations between Anglicans and Roman Catholics should be conducted with due regard to the multiplicity of conversations also in progress with other Churches. In them all we propose to hold fast the principles of Catholic truth as we have been given to understand them, though we realize that, in renewed obedience to the Holy Spirit, we must at all times be willing to go forward adventurously.

Reports of Anglican–Roman Catholic conversations in the several provinces should be made available to members of the Permanent Joint Commission, and information on all these matters circulated by it throughout our communion.

MIXED MARRIAGES

We are aware of the suffering which may arise from marriages in which one partner is an Anglican and the other a Roman Catholic, but welcome the fact that a Joint Commission on the Theology of Marriage and its Application to Mixed Marriages has been set up. The preliminary discussions of this joint commission have shown that the two Churches are close to one another in acknowledging that Holy Matrimony has a sacramental nature, although this is somewhat differently expressed in our respective formularies.

We welcome a suggestion from the (Roman Catholic) Third World Congress for the Lay Apostolate that Anglican priests should be acceptable as the official ministerial witnesses required by the Roman Catholic Church.

We note that the same Congress has asked that the responsibility for the Christian education of the children of a mixed marriage should be regarded as the responsibility of both parents who share in the grace of the marriage sacrament, and note that this is endorsed by the Declaration on Religious Liberty of Vatican II, which states: "Parents . . . have the right to determine, in accordance with their own religious beliefs, the kind of religious education that their children are to receive."

We also welcome the movement towards joint pastoral care of all concerned both before and after marriage by the clergy of the two Churches. Such joint pastoral care is an expression of the theology of Holy Matrimony which both Churches share.

## EPISCOPACY, COLLEGIALITY, PAPACY

The Anglican tradition has always regarded *episcopacy* as an essential part of its Catholic inheritance. We would regard it as an extension of the apostolic office and function both in time and space, and, moreover, we regard the transmission of apostolic power and responsibility as an activity of the college of bishops and never as a result of isolated action by any individual bishop.

In the discharge of his episcopal responsibility, the bishop is the guardian of the faith, the father of his people, and the driving force of mission in his area.

Traditionally the bishop is father in God to the clergy and laity of a territorial diocese, and part of his vocation is to represent the Catholic Church in his diocese and, conversely, to represent his diocese within the councils of the wider Church.

While we have no wish to diminish the importance of this traditional pattern, the demands of a new age suggest the wisdom of also consecrating bishops without territorial jurisdiction but with pastoral responsibility, directly or indirectly, for special groups such as the armed forces, industry, and particular areas of concern within the mission of the Church. This principle would simply be the extension of the widespread current practice of appointing suffragans, auxiliaries, and assistants. We submit that all such bishops, by virtue of their consecration as bishops in the Church of God, should have their due place in episcopal councils throughout the world.

The principle underlying *collegiality* is that the apostolic calling, responsibility, and authority are an inheritance given to the whole body or college of bishops. Every individual bishop has therefore a responsibility both as a member of this college and as chief pastor in his diocese. In the latter capacity he exercises direct oversight over the people committed to his charge. In the former he shares with his brother bishops throughout the world a concern for the wellbeing of the whole Church.

Within the college of bishops it is evident that there must be a president. In the Anglican Communion this position is at present held by the occupant of the historic see of Canterbury, who enjoys a primacy of honour, not of jurisdiction. This primacy is found to involve, in a particular way, that care for all the Churches which is shared by all the bishops.

The renewed sense of the collegiality of the episcopate is especially important at a time when most schemes for unity are being developed at a national level, because the collegiality of the episcopate helps to stress the worldwide and universal character of the Church. This collegiality must be a guiding principle in the growth of the relationships between the provinces of the Anglican Communion and those Churches with which we are, or shall be, in full communion. Within this larger college of bishops, the primacy would take on a new character which would need to be worked out in consultation with the Churches involved.

As a result of the emphasis placed on collegiality at the Second Vatican Council, the status of bishops in the Roman Catholic Church was in great measure enhanced, though the teaching of the First Vatican Council on the infallibility and immediate and universal jurisdiction of the Pope was unaffected. We are unable to accept this teaching as it is commonly understood today. The relationships between the Pope and the episcopal college, of which he is a member, are, however, still being clarified, and are subject to development. We recall the statement made in the Lambeth Conference of 1908, and repeated in 1920 and 1930, "that there can be no fulfilment of the Divine purpose in any scheme of reunion which does not ultimately include the great Latin Church of the West, with which our history has been so closely associated in the past, and to which we are still bound by many ties of common faith and tradition". We recognize the Papacy as a historic reality whose developing role requires deep reflection and joint study by all concerned for the unity of the whole Body of Christ.

Although the declaration and guardianship of the faith has traditionally been regarded as belonging fundamentally to the episcopal office, the collegiality of the episcopate must always be seen in the context of the conciliar character of the Church, involving the *consensus fidelium*, in which the episcopate has its place.

## RELATIONS WITH THE
## EASTERN ORTHODOX CHURCHES

Orthodox and Anglicans face alike in the current world such factors as:

1.  The diminished awareness of God and of the holy in modern life where, in an unsettled society, technological achievements have lessened man's sense of dependence on God.

2.  The persistence of nineteenth-century atheism as a basic political concept, not least in countries where the Orthodox faith is predominant, leading in places to a deliberate effort to establish societies without the concept of God.

PROGRESS

Since the last Lambeth Conference we have followed with great interest pan-Orthodox conferences in Rhodes in 1961 and 1964, in Belgrade in 1966, and in Geneva in 1968, and have noted with real satisfaction the visits of the Archbishop of Canterbury to Orthodox Patriarchs and their return visits to him, as well as exchanges of delegations with Moscow, Belgrade, and Bucharest. It is a matter of particular joy that a specific date is soon to be set for the resumption of pan-Orthodox and pan-Anglican discussions with the Orthodox begun in 1931, to which the Lambeth Conferences of 1948 and 1958 looked forward.

The Oriental (Orthodox) Churches held a conference in Addis Ababa in 1965. We warmly reciprocate their hope that our mutual esteem will lead to fruitful dialogue between our Churches.

The vastly increased number of Orthodox and Oriental Christians in Australia, Canada, Great Britain, and the United States has expanded considerably the scope not only for theological discussion but also for dialogue at the parochial level on common problems and enterprises. A growing awareness of the ways of the Orthodox has been stimulated by their welcome presence in the western world as well as by the great increase in the numbers of pilgrims and travellers to Jerusalem and the Orthodox East.

THE WAY AHEAD

Conscious of God's call to us to grasp the opportunities as well as to tackle the dangers in our present world, we urge Orthodox theologians and scholars to share increasingly with ours tasks of common concern, such as the following:

1.  Integration of modern biblical scholarship into a contemporary extension of the great patristic tradition, the tradition in which the Fathers brought the light of the latest culture of their day, its philosophy and science, to an understanding of the truths of revelation.

2.  Revitalization of a theology which is both fully Orthodox and at the same time contemporary, using modern modes of thought and expression to convey the reality of man's encounter with the facts of God's creation, incarnation, and redemption of the world. Such a reformulation should be the contemporary expression of our common commitment to the faith of the early, un-divided, ecumenical Church and of our determination to continue to present that faith in the future. In so doing we should hope increasingly to discover and recognize in each other's Churches the same Church of Christ and to find dogmatic and doctrinal agreement sufficient to warrant sacramental unity.

3. Consideration of the great social issues of the day such as economics, morals and medicine, and the just society.

4. Study of ways in which liturgical worship may become not only a service of spiritual edification and strengthening for our faithful in their present-day life, but also a service of inspiration for their mission in carrying out their daily witness to Christ in effective social involvement in the world of today. Such joint studies should seek also ways by which those who have become indifferent to the Christian faith may be stimulated to a turning of the mind and heart in response to God's love.

ANGLICAN AND ORTHODOX JOINT DOCTRINAL DISCUSSIONS

The pan-Orthodox conference at Belgrade in 1966 compiled a list of theological subjects for discussion with Anglicans. We welcome these and would wish especially to study with them such matters as the Filioque clause in the Nicene Creed, comprehensiveness, and matters that have arisen in this Conference.

(1) *The Filioque clause in the Nicene Creed.* The underlying theological issues will be dealt with in the projected Joint Doctrinal discussions. Meanwhile, the restoration of the Nicene Creed in a form omitting the Filioque should be carefully considered by Anglican provinces engaged in liturgical reform.

(2) *Comprehensiveness* is an attitude of mind which Anglicans have learned from the thought-provoking controversies of their history. We are grateful to the Orthodox for making us think once more what we mean by comprehensiveness, and shall be glad to study the matter afresh with their help; for we realize that we have been too ready to take it for granted. We offer the following reflections to aid discussion.

Comprehensiveness demands agreement on fundamentals, while tolerating disagreement on matters in which Christians may differ without feeling the necessity of breaking communion. In the mind of an Anglican, comprehensiveness is not compromise. Nor is it to bargain one truth for another. It is not a sophisticated word for syncretism. Rather it implies that the apprehension of truth is a growing thing: we only gradually succeed in "knowing the truth". It has been the tradition of Anglicanism to contain within one body both Protestant and Catholic elements. But there is a continuing search for the whole truth in which these elements will find complete reconciliation. Comprehensiveness implies a willingness to allow liberty of interpretation, with a certain slowness in arresting or restraining exploratory thinking. We tend to applaud the wisdom of the rabbi Gamaliel's dictum that if a thing is not of God it will not last very long (Acts 5.38-9). Moreover we are alarmed by the sad experience of too hasty condemnation in the past (as in the case of Galileo). For we believe that in leading us into all the truth the Holy Spirit may have some surprises in store for us in the future as he has had in the past. "The only authority in the Catholic Church which can ultimately preserve the truth is the power of the Holy Ghost to guide theologians in the end to a true understanding of the faith."[1]

Long before ecumenism became a household word strong ties of love and mutual respect had already bound us closely to our Orthodox brothers. Now in a changed and changing ecumenical climate we still cherish that intimacy and the shared appreciation of the glorious experience of being in Christ. This can fill with warm understanding a conversation together about bishops and their relationship to the other orders, presbyterate, diaconate, laity; about the role of primacies such as Papacy and Patriarchates within the overall consideration of authority, discipline, freedom, and the Holy Spirit's guidance of the Church; and other matters of current concern, including the recognition of ministries.

Since happily we now live side by side in so many parts of the world, we would encourage Orthodox and Anglican fellowship in worship (short of violation of sacramental disciplines), followed by opportunities for discussion, so that clergy and laity of both Churches may be brought to a better understanding of one another's tradition and see there the authentic notes of Christ's one, holy, catholic, and apostolic Church.

## THE ROLE OF THE ANGLICAN COMMUNION IN THE FAMILIES OF CHRISTENDOM

We recognize in penitence how often we fall short of our calling, in which we seek to base our faith and practice upon the Bible as understood by the traditions of the undivided Church and as illuminated by the Holy Spirit in every age. In particular we cherish, value, and use the two sacraments of the gospel, the Apostles' and Nicene Creeds, and the threefold ministry. In the worshipping life of our communion we share a common heritage of Prayer Books, themselves based upon the Bible.

We are a family of autonomous Churches, varied and flexible, linked by ties of history, tradition, and living fellowship with the see of Canterbury, the focal point of our communion.

In the face of God's majesty and love we often feel called to pursue a middle way, not as compromise but as a positive grasp of many-sided truth. We have come to value reason and tolerance and to be com-

---

[1]E. Milner-White and W. L. Knox, *One God and Father of All* (1929), p. 100.

prehensive even at the expense of strict logic. We are prepared to live, both in fellowship and in tension, with those who in some points differ from us.

The organization of Anglican Churches into provinces is helping us to understand our comprehensiveness and to have a wider vision of the richness of our communion.

AIMS OF ANGLICANISM

1. To welcome, encourage, and be ready to give counsel in the merging of Anglican Churches in united national or regional Churches.

2. To enter into full communion with all such united Churches, even while certain anomalies remain.

3. To maintain support of such united Churches, as well as to support one another, Church and Church in the Anglican Communion, as need and opportunity arise, with spiritual, intellectual, and material assistance; and to take common counsel.

4. To preserve and enrich our special insights, and to contribute them to the whole Christian Church and to the world.

We believe that the Anglican witness and the Anglican role will continue; but the processes of church union will mean that the frontiers of Anglicanism become less defined. Our Anglican contribution to Christendom will be made partly through a closely knit communion and partly through co-operation and fellowship with others. We believe that the concept of "communion with the see of Canterbury" affords a sacramental link of abiding value.

We believe that it would be premature to seek to define now the future relations between the Anglican Churches and the united Churches which will include former Anglican provinces or dioceses. In this process there will be a fruitful sharing and interpenetration of many traditions, as the Anglican Communion affirms and merges its own insights of faith and order in each new expression of the one, holy, catholic, and apostolic Church.

We also regard full participation of the various provinces and regions of the Anglican Communion in the consultations and work of the World Council of Churches and in their promotion of joint action for mission as of vital importance. Every opportunity of dialogue and co-operation with other communions should be welcomed. Concern with specific Anglican structures or with the concept of wider episcopal fellowships must not exclude the widest possible ecumenical involvement.

SPECIFIC PROBLEMS IN CONNECTION WITH OUR ROLE

*Worldwide Anglican–Lutheran Dialogue*

In January 1968 an Anglican–Lutheran Committee appointed by the Archbishop of Canterbury and the general secretary of the Lutheran World Federation suggested that there should be Anglican–Lutheran consultations at world level, and asked for the guidance of the Lambeth Conference.

We note that such conversations, in view of their influence upon national or regional union plans, might be expedient with other world confessional bodies. We recommend, however, that this particular suggestion, which originated with the Assembly of the Lutheran World Federation in 1963, should be accepted and acted upon forthwith; though recognizing that this would be in addition to very fruitful contacts already made in some regions.

The reasons for our recommendation are:

(a) We desire to respond to Lutheran ecumenical initiative.

(b) There are many historical, doctrinal, liturgical, and other bonds between our two communions.

(c) In local negotiations for unity both Lutherans and Anglicans tend to feel the need to refer questions to their whole communion.

(d) Lutheran–Roman Catholic conversations are already taking place, paralleling those between Anglicans and Roman Catholics; simultaneous Anglican–Lutheran conversations would be all the more effective.

We specifically recommend, therefore, that

(a) Anglican–Lutheran conversations should be held on four occasions over a two-year period. Such conversations need not entail excessive cost either in time or money.

(b) There should be not less than seven representatives on each side of diverse background and experience, not entirely theologians or of the clergy.

(c) The conversations should begin by discussing the general mission of the Church in the world and only afterwards proceed to questions of doctrine and order, though major issues should be faced as soon as possible.

*The Anglican Mission in Latin America*

In May 1968 the Conference of Anglican Bishops in South America asked the Lambeth Conference to look afresh at the Anglican mission in Latin America.

It is our conviction that our Anglican contribution is sorely needed both as an additional Christian presence and because of the special character of our communion.

We endorse therefore the general terms of the separate Resolution presented to the Conference by the Latin American bishops.

## The Anglican Presence in Europe

In May 1968 the general secretaries of the Church of England missionary societies asked the Lambeth Conference to give guidance about the direction in which Anglican activity in Europe should move. Over several centuries this work has grown naturally to meet the needs of Anglicans permanently or temporarily resident on the Continent. It includes the outstanding work of the Missions to Seamen. It involves ministry among the armed forces. There is a continuing need to minister to short-term visitors. These activities have been partly under the jurisdiction of the Bishops of Gibraltar and Fulham, partly under Bishops of the Episcopal Church of the United States. To some extent the work has reflected national loyalties rather than the Anglican Communion as a whole. It must be understood that what follows is written in deep appreciation of past and present Anglican work in Europe.

We have a continuing duty to minister to Anglicans in Europe, but it is not our policy to develop Anglicanism as a separate confessional body on the Continent. We look forward to the time when Anglicans in Europe will develop even closer relations with one or other of the Christian Churches in the countries where they reside. Where, in any particular area, there is a Church in full communion with us, we should work for a closer integration of existing ministries and congregations, even to the extent of entrusting our work to them.

We regard the existence of parallel jurisdictions as deplorable, and think that this problem should be resolved as soon as possible. We suggest that the proposed Anglican Consultative Council should arrange further consultations between the Church of England and the Episcopal Church of the United States. We recommend that the Old Catholic Churches, the Spanish Reformed Episcopal Church, and the Lusitanian Church of Portugal be invited to participate.

## Parallel Jurisdictions

The cohesion and effectiveness of the Anglican Communion in various parts of the world, e.g. West Africa, the Caribbean area, and Latin America, are adversely affected by the existence of parallel jurisdictions. We suggest that the Anglican Consultative Council should give early consideration to these problems.

## The Anglican Presence in Geneva

It has been suggested that there should be an Anglican Centre in Geneva, in view of the fact that the World Council of Churches and various world confessional bodies have their headquarters in that city. It is our opinion that the need for this Centre can be adequately supplied for the present by a joint strengthening of the existing American and English chaplaincies.

## INTER-ANGLICAN STRUCTURES

The growing together of Christians has brought the Churches of the Anglican Communion to a new stage in their relations with one another and with other Churches and organizations. We appreciate the work hitherto done by the Lambeth Consultative Body, by the Advisory Council on Missionary Strategy, and, more recently, by the office of the Anglican Executive Officer and his advisory committee; but we believe that a more integrated pattern is now necessary, in which, as "members severally one of another", Anglicans may fulfil their common inter-Anglican and ecumenical responsibilities in promoting the unity, renewal, and mission of Christ's Church.

We therefore propose the formation of an *Anglican Consultative Council*, which would continue the responsibilities hitherto entrusted to the L.C.B. and the A.C.M.S., and the replacement of the office of the Anglican Executive Officer by a Secretary General appointed by, and responsible to, the Council.

The constitution of the proposed Council is printed as a schedule to Resolution 69.

The Section also recommends that:

1.  In view of the historic importance of the *Lambeth Conference* over the past hundred years and the undoubted value of the present meeting, the Archbishop of Canterbury should be asked to decide, on the advice of the Anglican Consultative Council, upon the calling of future Conferences and on their time, place, and agenda.

2.  *Worldwide Anglican Congresses* should be replaced by:

    (a)  *a joint meeting*, at the time of an Assembly of the World Council of Churches, *of the Consultative Council and of Anglican participants in the Assembly* in or near the place where the Assembly is held. This Anglican meeting should receive a report from the Consultative Council on its work and on that of the Secretary General and should consider other matters brought to it by the Council.

    (b)  *regional meetings* of representatives of Anglican Churches, if possible in association with meetings of Area Councils of Churches.

3.  The office of *Regional Officer* should be discontinued, but regional Churches should be ready to allow their *qualified staff* to col-

laborate with the office and work of the Secretary General, especially in the field of study and research.

4. (a) The appreciation of the Conference be recorded of the progress made in the use of *The Cycle of Prayer for the Anglican Communion* and *Response,* and of the collaboration that has developed in the last five years between those responsible in several Anglican Churches for their production.

   (b) The use of *A Cycle of Prayer for Anglican Use* (as it will be called from 1969 onwards) and *Response* be warmly commended to the clergy and laity of the Anglican Communion.

   (c) The Consultative Council be requested to keep the progress of these publications under review and to encourage consultation with other well-tried schemes of Bible reading and intercession such as the Bible Reading Fellowship and the Scripture Union.

5. In view of the undue dependence of *the World Council of Churches* on North American generosity, the other member Churches of our Communion should examine, in collaboration with other W.C.C. members in their area, the adequacy of their contributions and, so far as possible, increase them; and the Consultative Council should keep under review the level of contributions from the member Churches of the Anglican Communion to the World Council of Churches.

6. Inasmuch as *Mutual Responsibility and Interdependence in the Body of Christ* (M.R.I.) has proved to be a great inspiration and blessing, the concept and programme should be continued. In particular, the project system should be pursued, subject to the following comments:

   (a) Each Church must be free to decide to what extent it is appropriate to its own needs.

   (b) Project programmes should be realistic in scale, flexible in operation, and in harmony with accepted criteria.

   (c) Account should be taken in all building projects not only of the original capital cost but also of the continuing cost of maintenance.

   (d) Support of the local ordained ministry should be a first charge of the local Church and not normally included in a Directory of Projects. The Directory, however, might be used to facilitate the interchange of personnel between regional Churches on a short-term basis.

(e) Regional Churches should be encouraged to appoint someone from their own membership, or to invite the Secretary General to send a representative, competent to help them in deciding on priorities among projects and in the effective planning, conduct, and evaluation of those selected.

## THE POSITIVE IDEA OF A WIDER EPISCOPAL FELLOWSHIP

Convinced as we are that God is still speaking today to his Church throughout the world, we have no doubt of our own responsibilities both to hear what he is saying and obediently to play whatever part is allotted to us Anglicans in the fulfilment of Christ's mandate for unity. We cannot know where the Holy Spirit will lead the Church a century hence, but we do know that under his guidance we must co-operate fully with all our Christian brethren in carrying out his mission to the world. Furthermore, it is our prayer that, as the work of unity goes forward, new Churches will be formed which can no longer be described in a limiting sense as Anglican but which will belong with us in a wider fellowship, sharing both the integrity of the faith and the historic episcopate in its various forms.

The Lambeth Conference of 1948, in Resolution 74, recommended that "bishops of the Anglican Communion and bishops of other Churches which are, or may be, in communion with them should meet together from time to time as an episcopal conference, advisory in character, for brotherly counsel and encouragement". Lambeth 1958 reaffirmed and elaborated this and strongly recommended the holding of such a conference.

Accordingly, a conference of this nature was held in 1964 at the invitation of the Archbishop of Canterbury with thirty-nine archbishops and bishops present representing the following Churches: the Anglican Churches, the Church of Finland, the Spanish Reformed Episcopal Church, the Lusitanian Church of Portugal, the Mar Thoma Syrian Church, the Old Catholic Churches, the Philippine Independent Catholic Church, the Polish National Catholic Church of America, the Church of South India, and the Church of Sweden.

With the general purpose and intent lying behind the resolutions of Lambeth 1948 and 1958, we are in agreement, stressing particularly the phrases "advisory in character" and "for brotherly counsel and encouragement".

We make two specific recommendations:

1. that a General Episcopal Consultation (on a worldwide scale) be held in the near future. Such a General Episcopal Consultation would meet on the initiative of the Archbishop of Canterbury,

with invitations to be sent primarily to those Churches possessing bishops which are in full or partial communion with Canterbury or other provinces of the Anglican Communion.

2.    that strong encouragement be given by this Lambeth Conference for the holding of Regional Episcopal Consultations on a wider basis of representation than suggested for the General Episcopal Consultation, under such local auspices and arrangements as seem appropriate and helpful in each region.

We believe that these recommendations would serve in setting forward the hopes expressed by the Archbishop of Canterbury for "a comity of bishops in the Church of God, both from ancient and from 'younger' Churches, who find their sharing in the bishop's office to be a ground of present partnerships and an anticipation of future collegial unity in the one universal Church".

## CONCLUSION

We believe that a deepened penitence for the creation and maintenance of divisions must show amendment by a life of common prayer and Bible study, and by friendship and service at every level, official and unofficial, local and national. With this in mind, the Section has therefore proposed to the Conference the adoption of Resolution 44. It is in such practical ways that we give reality to our words about the renewal of our unity in holiness and truth.

✠ LAKDASA CALCUTTA
*Chairman*

OBSERVERS

CONSULTANTS

INDEX

# Official Observers

## ARMENIAN CHURCH
CATHOLICOSSATE OF ETCHMIADZIN
The Most Rev. Archbishop Bessak Toumayan

CATHOLICOSSATE OF CILICIA
The Rt Rev. Bishop Karekin Sarkissian

## ASSEMBLIES OF GOD
Dr Thomas F. Zimmerman

## BAPTIST WORLD ALLIANCE
The Rev. Dr C. Ronald Goulding
The Rev. Dr Ernest A. Payne

## CHURCH OF SOUTH INDIA
The Rev. Dr Russell Chandran
The Rt Rev. Dr Lesslie Newbigin
The Most Rev. Pereji Solomon

## COPTIC CHURCH
The Rt Rev. Bishop Athanasius

## EVANGELICAL CHURCH IN GERMANY
The Rt Rev. Dr Hanns Lilje
*Oberkonsistorialrat Rev. Dr F. Schlingensiepen

## INTERNATIONAL CONGREGATIONAL COUNCIL
The Rev. Dr Norman Goodall
The Rev. John Huxtable

## LUSITANIAN CHURCH
The Rt Rev. Dr Luís C. R. Pereira

## LUTHERAN WORLD FEDERATION

The Rt Rev. Dr Fridtjov Birkeli
The Rev. Dr Keith R. Bridston
The Most Rev. Dr Gunnar A. E. Hultgren
The Rev. Dr Harding Meyer
The Most Rev. Dr Martti Simojoki
*The Rev. Dr Åke Andrén
*The Rev. Dr Martin L. Kretzmann
*The Rev. Dr Jacob Kumaresan
*The Rev. Dr Einar Molland
*The Rev. Dr Martti Parvio
*The Rev. Dr Regin Prenter
**The Rt Rev. Bengt Sundkler

## MAR THOMA CHURCH

The Rt Rev. Philipose Mar Chrysostom

## OLD CATHOLIC CHURCH

The Most Rev. Dr Andreas Rinkel
*The Rt Rev. Josef Brinkhues
*The Rt Rev. Gerhardus A. van Kleef

## ORTHODOX CHURCH

CONSTANTINOPLE
The Most Rev. Archbishop Athenagoras of Thyateira
**Professor Basil Anagnostopoulos

ALEXANDRIA
The Most Rev. Metropolitan Parthenios of Carthage

JERUSALEM
The Very Rev. Archimandrite Cornelios Rodoussakis

MOSCOW
The Most Rev. Archbishop Antony of Minsk and Byelorussia

SERBIA
The Rt Rev. Bishop Firmilian

ROMANIA
The Rt Rev. Bishop Antim of Tîrgoviste

BULGARIA

The Most Rev. Metropolitan Nicodim of Sliven

CYPRUS

The Rt Rev. Bishop Kallinicos of Amathus

ORTHODOX CHURCH OF FRANCE AND WESTERN EUROPE

The Very Rev. Archimandrite Alexandre Semenoff-Tian-Chansky

RUSSIAN ORTHODOX CHURCH IN EXILE

The Very Rev. Archpriest Count Leonid Ignatiew

## PHILIPPINE INDEPENDENT CATHOLIC CHURCH

The Most Rev. Isabelo de los Reyes
**The Rt Rev. Camilo C. Diel
**The Rt Rev. Macario V. Ga

## RELIGIOUS SOCIETY OF FRIENDS

Douglas V. Steere

## ROMAN CATHOLIC CHURCH

The Rt Rev. Mgr Peter J. Butelezi, O.M.I.
The Rt Rev. Dom Christopher Butler, O.S.B.
The Rev. Fr John Coventry, S.J.
The Most Rev. Remi J. De Roo
The Very Rev. Canon William Purdy
The Rev. Dr Herbert J. Ryan, S.J.
The Rt Rev. Mgr J. G. M. Willebrands
*The Most Rev. William Z. Gomes
*The Rt Rev. Thomas Holland
**The Rt Rev. Mgr Jean-François Arrighi
**The Very Rev. Canon Josef A. Dessain
**The Very Rev. Dom Philibert Zobel, O.S.B.

## SALVATION ARMY

Commissioner Herbert Westcott
*Brigadier William G. Brown

## SPANISH REFORMED EPISCOPAL CHURCH

The Rt Rev. Ramón Taibo

## SYRIAN ORTHODOX CHURCH

The Most Rev. Mar Severius Zakka Iwas

WORLD CONVENTION OF CHURCHES OF CHRIST
The Rev. Dr George G. Beazley Jr

WORLD COUNCIL OF CHURCHES
The Rev. Dr Eugene Carson Blake
Dr Nikos A. Nissiotis
*The Very Rev. Archpriest Vitaly M. Borovoi
*The Rev. Steven G. Mackie
*The Rev. Dr Lukas Vischer

WORLD METHODIST COUNCIL
The Rev. Bishop Fred P. Corson
The Rev. A. Raymond George
The Rev. Bishop Odd Hagen
The Rev. Dr Harold Roberts

WORLD PRESBYTERIAN ALLIANCE
The Rev. Arthur L. MacArthur
The Rev. Dr James I. McCord
The Rev. Dr Wilhelm Niesel
The Rev. Dr William Stewart

*Invitations were sent to the following Churches but Observers were not present:*
CHURCH OF THE EAST (ASSYRIAN)
ETHIOPIAN CHURCH
ORTHODOX PATRIARCHATES OF ANTIOCH AND
GEORGIA AND THE CHURCH OF GREECE

*Alternate Observers
**Special Guest Observers

# Consultants

The Rev. A. M. Allchin

Dr P. B. Anderson

Miss E. M. Batten, O.B.E.

The Ven. E. F. Carpenter

The Rev. Professor H. Chadwick

The Rev. Canon A. K. Cragg

The Rev. H. F. J. Daniel

Dr Peter Day

The Rev. Professor E. Fairweather

The Rev. Canon J. Findlow

Dr W. C. Fletcher

The Rev. E. M. B. Green

The Rev. Fr. M. Jarrett-Kerr, C.R.

The Rev. Canon D. E. Jenkins

The Rev. J. Luwum

The Rev. Professor J. Macquarrie

The Rev. J. Mbiti

The Rev. Canon B. S. Moss

The Rev. Professor D. E. Nineham

The Rev. Canon D. M. Paton

The Rev. C. Powles

The Rev. Professor H. E. Root

The Rt Rev. R. R. Roseveare, S.S.M.

The Rev. Canon J. R. Satterthwaite

The Rev. Canon J. V. Taylor

The Rev. Canon D. Webster

# Index